Misery to Victory

The Pathway to Finding lasting peace

Samuel Johnson

authorHOUSE®

AuthorHouse™
1663 Liberty Drive
Bloomington, IN 47403
www.authorhouse.com
Phone: 833-262-8899

Published by AuthorHouse   09/08/2023

ISBN: 979-8-8230-1404-5 (sc)
ISBN: 979-8-8230-1403-8 (hc)
ISBN: 979-8-8230-1402-1 (e)

Library of Congress Control Number: 2023916594

Print information available on the last page.

This book is printed on acid-free paper.

Contents

Dedication vii

Prologue ix

Introduction xiii

My Life Journey: The Chaos and the Calm 1

Genesis: The Sad Beginning of an Innocent Boy 7

My Mother: Savage and Egocentric 11

My Childhood 15

Boarding School: Love Is Where You Least Expect It 17

My College Years 21

Marriage and Divorce: My New Life 25

Tales of My Wife's Twaddle: My Nonbiological Second Daughter ... 29

The Mind of Evil and Chaos: How My Ex-Wife Thinks 33

Finding the Angel 37

Israel: Home like No Other 55

Life after Divorce 59

The Investigation 63

Sarah 67

Priscilla—A Breath of Fresh Air 69

Priscilla's Kids 77

Lessons Learned through Lack of Trust and Blown Fortunes 79

Epilogue 85

Conclusion 89

Dedication

I feel deep in my heart that I want to dedicate this book to my wife, Priscilla, and her kids. Priscilla changed my life and made life enjoyable as it had never been before. I had never experienced this much peace and happiness since I was born. I'm so glad I gave love a chance again. I appreciate her kids, who, although they are not my biological kids, have shown me respect and love deserving of a father. I didn't know what it meant to be happy and to have a family I could consistently depend on until I met Priscilla. We lived in bliss, and this beautiful family made me a better person. I am full of joy. I wake up to an adrenaline rush every morning. I feel joy, happiness, and being loved and cherished.

I am full of life and confident that my path is clear because I have this lovely family. I know I am not alone, and we can rise to meet any challenge together in the bliss of love and togetherness. I am more than satisfied to have found this beautiful woman. The day I found her is the day I found peace. I am grateful for this love and rarity of this connection. Thanks to Priscilla, I have become a family man, well respected by her and her kids. I enjoy giving and receiving from my family. In a way, I feel that it was worth living through my previous turbulent life so my life could end in such a wonderful way.

Prologue

We all have stories to tell, and life gives us the opportunity every day to add a new page to the memories of our lives. We meet different people from different walks of life who also feature in our stories. They are like the crew in our movies, and regardless of their professions or possessions, their interaction with us leaves imprints. Our relationships often define the quality and strength of our lives; they define our perspective toward life and the positions of our minds. The people we meet either break us or make us. I spent the first forty-four years of my life with people who wanted to break me. Life was a continuous streak of frustration, pain, sadness, and challenges, and oftentimes this translated to depression.

We are all of different races, colors, and backgrounds, and this may account for the differences in the challenges that we face. Even where we are identical in these traits, there are unique differences in our challenges. Some people would do anything to gain victory as long as the referee can raise his hands and declare them winners, and a crowd of people can cheer them up. Others wouldn't take defeat even with the blows these challenges rained on them. Even with the blows, they would get back up as if, underneath each blow, they hear a whisper that encourages them—a whisper only their ears can hear. Many more will quit without even trying.

I was broken, but I refused to remain on the floor. I got up with my body writhing in pain each time, but I didn't allow defeat in the ring. My desire grew even more; it became somewhat untamed with my desire to see life, feel love, live life, and overcome challenges.

This book is my story. I share how I went from consistent pain to gain, from peril to peace, from a life full of sad, sleepless nights to a life full of glee. I have come, to live my dream of happiness and tranquility.

My story might make you cry, and I don't mean to upset you, but you will also learn that you can come back from anything; you will find out that you can always get to your destination once you keep moving. I will share how I was born into despair and went through the gutters of life to get to where I am today.

My life started on the wrong foot, putting me in an environment where I was unwanted without compromise in words and actions. My story can encourage others to keep going and never give up hope for a better life. Everything in this book is based on real events in my life, from birth to age seventy.

From birth to age three, I was told only many stories. From age three to forty-four, I woke up every morning wishing that day would be my last day. I wished the pain would go away, but it never did. When you read and learn all about my life, you will agree. I was born to a mother who cursed the day she learned her fourth child was another boy and not a girl. She wanted the features of a female child, but she got what she was used to seeing—a male child with wails so loud that it pierced the hospital walls and, obviously, her heart. My mother's disappointment followed me throughout my childhood and then through life. I felt vulnerable, and I succumbed to do her biding just to get a little love from her, just so that she could like me.

On most days, I cried harder than I had the previous day. I would curl up into a ball and cry myself to sleep. Only the rays of the sun and the singing birds would make me know that morning had come. My heart ached a lot, and I carried scars too deep for a child to bear. I naively believed they would fade away with time, but even more frighteningly, as I gradually grew up and became a man, they started to define who I was against my wishes.

I needed a world where I would be seen and appreciated. I began to look outside the doors of my father's mansion, but I still couldn't find that appreciation. I grew more scared by the minute; the tickling of the clock confirmed my fears as I sank deeper into what I thought my mother had a better understanding of. I was better off dead than alive.

She had said so several times, and I was starting to believe it. Even more deadly, I was taking steps toward making my life end sooner rather than later. It was going to be recorded as a suicide, so I didn't need much to plot it. A little cut here and there should do the trick, but I couldn't get it right every time.

I learned what love is all about from an aunt who frequently came to take care of me when my parents were away. She taught me clear pictures of love that I began to find interesting; this was something I had never experienced before. I wanted what my aunt had, but I didn't know how to get it while living in a mentally exhausting home.

My determination grew, and I resolved to find it no matter what. To do this, I would have to leave the comfort and security. I had to transform from the son to a man. The road was rough, and I have many scars to prove it, but I think I have found what I was looking for.

This book mainly describes the process of a lifetime that forced me to develop into a great person and a unique personality.

These lifetime processes put me in a school where I learned—and am still learning—that nothing is lost in life. There is always a new life in which you can find the happiness and balance you want as you position yourself for the best.

As you read this book, you will have reasons to believe that you can come back from anything, and you will see reasons to want to try again. I did not write this book to seek sympathy. I want to use my story to teach people that, to find where you are wanted and loved, you have to leave where you are unwanted.

Introduction

This book describes my life as an Israeli man who had nothing but a lousy blessing from day one. Most of the energy I experienced made my life hell on earth. Although life was horrible, my experiences made me a super survivor. Every time I had a new start during my life, I was taking another step toward something that ended for the better. As I look back at my difficulties, it seems to me that God wanted to find out how much I could take. I suffered day in and out for over sixty years.

The book describes how my mother took all her frustration out on me and how I was treated poorly and unfairly by my siblings. My family—my mother and my older brothers and especially my sister—contributed to most of the pain I lived with as a child. I would not have expected it at the time, but I believe this pain defined my perspective of life and my personality.

This is a story of my difficult, miserable childhood. I lived a vulnerable life. I was raised in so much fear that, by the time I felt I needed to find the love I deserved, my experiences had clouded my knowledge of what love should be. When I found a woman to marry, I thought she would give me all the love I needed and make me feel special, but she was evil and cruel and practically wiped me out of everything. I lived with her for sixteen years in the United States, and I worked hard, but this woman took all I had and even took away my three beloved children. I ended up having a terrible first marriage, which I still blindly did everything to save. I had to admit that I didn't know what love was, so I was not able to give enough of it. I wanted to get my definitions clear and pour all I found love to be on myself, so for my peace, I eventually left. I am sharing this story because I may have been through hell, and maybe others are going through the same, and they might draw motivation from my story.

The last part of the book is the good part. I share the story of how my life turned for the better. That happened when I found a woman who was a totally different person from the first two women I had known and grown old with. I imagine that there must be others who have experienced similar troubles. Hopefully, this will help them to see reasons to keep fighting and trying again.

Life is one precious thing that no one should let go of. Once you read my stories, you will appreciate that there is a reason to live life and go for the best life has to offer.

Believe me, life may seem unfair, but if you learn how to control situations around you, you will get better at this game and have good memories to hold onto and a blissful life to lead.

My Life Journey: The Chaos and the Calm

I wrote this poem before I went to boarding school while I was in so much pain and filled with surprise because of the way I was being treated. It is a long one, but it encapsulates how I felt and how determined I was to fight back for the kind of life I wanted, regardless of the circumstances.

> A chaotic life, a swirling storm,
> Never a moment to feel happy.
> From home and abroad
> and back again,
> No love found.
> No room for joy, no space for peace.
> A constant battle, a never-ending race.
> No time to breathe, no time to embrace
> The beauty of life, the love around—
> Just chaos and noise, a constant sound.
> But in the chaos, I find my strength,
> A fire inside that won't extinguish.
> I'll keep on fighting through the fray;
> I'll find my peace, come what may.
> For in the chaos, I am alive,
> A warrior fighting to survive.
> And though the journey may be tough,
> I'll keep on going. I've had enough
> Of living life in disarray.

I'll find my balance, come what may,
And in the calm, I'll find my way
To a life of peace, a brighter day.

I grew up in Israel and lived there until I turned twenty-three, when I moved to the United States and lived there for twenty-one years. At the age of forty-four, I returned to my native country and learned how to live a new life altogether.

My change in environment involved facing various challenges and setbacks, such as financial struggles, language barriers, and feeling homesick and isolated. However, starting life from zero can also be a rewarding and enriching experience, and I have done it several times. Change provided me with the opportunity to learn new skills, meet new people, and discover new interests and passions. I was given second and third chances, and I had to develop resilience, adaptability, and independence as I learned to navigate new situations and overcome obstacles. Starting life from zero can be a mix of excitement, uncertainty, challenges, and feelings of accomplishment and growth. For me, changes contributed to a challenging but ultimately fulfilling journey.

I learned the values of life and how to be strong in all aspects of life, no matter what I faced. I remember seeing a bumper sticker in the United States that said "Life's a bitch, and then you die." Another one read "Life's a bitch, and then you marry one." I found them funny because I didn't expect them to play out in my story. It was just some sad joke from some people experiencing emotional breakdown. I was on a quest to find love, and only true love was available on the streets of New York.

Then, bad luck, I married a woman who was very like my mother. She manipulated and abused me as my mother had done. This story could benefit those who feel that life is not "fair." It is for people who don't understand why life is cruel to them. People are good at giving bits of advice, but many don't know what it is like to go through such a life. My stories are from my real-life events, which took place in real time.

My ex-wife and I spent sixteen years together. They were sixteen miserable years. At about forty-four years old, I was viciously thrown out of my house and away from my children. My wife made the decision to divorce me.

At that time, I returned to my native country and started a new life again. Whatever I thought I had built wasn't there anymore, and no matter how hard I tried, I knew I would never get it back. My wealth had been given to my wife as a recompense for the years she claimed I wasted in her life.

From this point, I started life all over again at zero; it was not the first time in my life I would have to start all over again.

Those moments were the most difficult for me because I realized that life can be beautiful, but at other times, it can be just more suffering. The episodes were repetitive for me. I would experience a season of comfort, and then it would be as if I got robbed, tied up, and thrown out into an entirely different space. All I had gathered would fizzle out again. I had had to retrace my path to look carefully at the mistakes I might have made and pick myself up again. This happened several times throughout my life, and yet, against all odds, I pulled through. Later in my life, I met several other women, and although our relationships did not materialize into long-term associations, they did not cause the pain caused by my ex-wife or my mother.

Finally, I met a lovely woman. We married and now have a wonderful life as a family together. I never understood what love was all about or what it felt like because, so I often, I had fallen into traps of deceitful women who wanted only a taste of what I had built. I wasn't shown love and care except when I was left with my aunt who watched over me when my parents took trips around Europe. My aunt had a special place in my heart that I would always hold dear because, with her, I had a glimpse of what love is all about. Perhaps, if I had spent more time with her other than her visits only when my parents weren't around, I would have learned more.

Most of the things I learned from my aunt came from her actions rather than her words. I could make a list of what I learned about what love should be. My aunt was not one to hide her feelings toward me. She openly gave me hugs and kisses even when we were outside of the house, and that made me first question if it was appropriate. Don't blame me; I was naïve. I knew that love is a complex mix of emotions, behaviors, and beliefs associated with strong feelings of affection, protectiveness, warmth, and respect for another person. It has multifaceted sides and can be expressed in various ways, including actions, words, and physical connections. It can be characterized by tenderness, generosity, and selflessness as well as by passion and commitment.

My aunt cared a lot about me, so I knew love should involve caring for, supporting, and respecting another person. It also should involve a choice to put another's needs above your own. It can also involve sharing common interests, values, and goals. It is a powerful force that inspires and motivates people to do great things. It involves sacrificing your well-being for the well-being of the person you love. It can bring joy, happiness, security, and belonging. However, love can also bring challenges and difficulties. Effort, compromise, and open communication are required to maintain and strengthen the bond between two people. Love can also be complex and difficult to define, as it can take many forms and meanings.

Despite its complexities, love is an essential human experience that plays a central role in many people's lives. It can bring people together, create strong emotional bonds, and provide comfort, support, and happiness.

I had never felt love before. I had felt only pain and anger; not even my mom could show me love. I had never felt love for anyone except for my aunt, who loved me as she loved her own two sons. She treated me with so much love and compassion that any onlookers must have thought I was hers.

I wrote all these things in my journal and was on the lookout for someone to whom I could express love. One thing I didn't take the time to observe, though, was that my aunt had so much love inside her to give. To be like her, I had to have so much love inside of me that I could give it out, but I was a shattered boy! How on earth could I do that!

As a man, I was too quick to mistake some people's attitudes for love, so the moment anyone treated me differently, I danced to their tune till I realized that we weren't speaking the same language.

I am away now from my three lovely children. I devoted my life to my children for sixteen years and endured the torture caused by living with a woman I wouldn't wish on my enemies. I saw the warning flags, and it would have been better to end my marriage the moment I discovered the first lie about her, but I had to keep my wife and marriage because of my children. Every day, I woke up with the hope that our relationship would change for the better.

My children now don't even respond to my emails, and they block me on all social media platforms available. This is due to my ex-wife's alienation over the years. I am a divorced dad; my ex-wife does all she can to make my kids hate me. It satisfies her own sick needs to continue her way of abusing me and neglecting my feelings.

I have been away from my kids for twenty-five years; they have suffered throughout these years while I learned to continue my life. As I mentioned, I restarted life from "point zero" several times throughout my life. I just wish my kids knew the truth, but I wasn't around them. I wasn't permitted to be close to them to let them in on all that my marriage to their mother had been. I don't even think they would believe me.

My life's journey may sound familiar to other people who have gone through similar challenges in life. I know that many people face the same or similar circumstances. My story can help others see that they're not the only ones in this world who go through these trials. They are not alone in their challenges, and they can definitely pull through if they don't give up hope and keep pushing as hard as they can. There were times when I felt as if I didn't have the strength to push again. You may feel same way right now. But guess what I did? I sat down and waited till I had enough strength to push again!

You should have the mentality that life is for fighters, and you are one of the best! As you read through my stories, you can take advantage of the lessons I learned, knowing that life can be great regardless of the suffering involved.

Life made me develop a different personality from the one I possessed when I was a child. I was soft on the inside but thick on the outside. I never showed my emotions; no one knew when I was hurt, in pain, or sad. That was the only way I knew how to survive. I built up an immunity to all kinds of suffering—physical, emotional, and mental. I became rigid about anything that would cause me emotional stress by practicing self-care; I alone cared for my well-being. I began to focus on my schoolwork, getting enough sleep, eating a healthy diet, exercising regularly, and engaging in activities I enjoyed.

I identified healthy coping mechanisms such as meditation, which helped me manage stress healthily. It was also important for me to cultivate a positive attitude by focusing on the positive aspects of my life and cultivating an attitude of gratitude. This helped me turn away from negative situations and build resilience.

Surround yourself with supportive people you can talk to about your feelings and who can offer emotional support. Also, if you are struggling to manage stress on your own, consider seeking the help of a mental health professional. A therapist or counselor can help you develop coping strategies and work through any underlying issues contributing to your stress.

Remember that building immunity to emotional stress takes time and effort. It's important to be patient with yourself and prioritize self-care and stress management.

Genesis: The Sad Beginning of an Innocent Boy

Expectations must have been high when my mother was pregnant with her fourth child. The three previous having been boys, she went from store to store getting little pink dresses, cute hair bows, and princess gowns. There were no ultrasound machines then, so there was nothing to prepare her for what was to come. I was born a boy instead of her hoped-for girl, putting all her happy plans to a waste. I never knew what ever happened to all the girl baby clothes she had bought or even if I had clothes to wear after I was born.

My mother cursed the day I was born a boy, not a girl. Early on, I was too young to understand. I was like every child who wanted succor and comfort from his mother, but I noticed that mine wasn't forthcoming. I would cry to be carried, but she wouldn't carry me. Unfortunately, my mother took all her frustration out on me while I was growing up. Imagine a baby who was hated by his mom the minute he was born. Imagine growing up cursed every day because your birth gender disappointed your mom. Growing up with my mother was a challenge from the start. She never approved of anything I did; neither did I ever hear a word of encouragement at things I did pretty well. Everything I did was just another episode of her making me understand that she didn't want me around. That always discouraged me.

This book will teach you how anyone with effort and determination can make it through life. It is easy to give up, yet there are many important reasons to hold on.

I went through hell until a late age when I started building self-confidence. I was the fourth of my mother's four boys, and I always wondered what I did differently from the other three that angered her so. I would try to talk like them, walk like them and even wear their clothes sometimes, but the reactions I received from my mother were still the same. Can you imagine trying to survive with such a mother? My mother finally gave birth to a girl—my kid sister—but too much damage had been done to me by then. There was so much damage, there was almost no hope for reconstruction.

I needed to separate my mother's voice from the tiny voice that said he loved me and called me a unique child. My teachers at school constantly said that too, but I needed to hear it from my mother before I could believe it. It never came. She would say hurtful things to me because I was not the gender she wanted. How could a mother be like that?

I longed to have the fairytale life I read about in storybooks. I imagined a fairy godmother appearing to help me somehow, someday, but I wasn't a girl. But maybe it doesn't matter; boys could have fairy godmothers. She would dress me up as a prince and take me away from my mother's kingdom to my own. My mother would beg me to stay and say she was sorry for all the evil things she had done to me. For a child, I had quite a wild imagination, but it was soon killed by my mother. Finally, I didn't think the fairy godmother would come, but deep down, I hoped.

Circumstances in my life encouraged me to develop a unique personality, the kind of personality only people who go through hell embrace. I am a survivor in every meaning of the word; I learned to become a brick. The negative words came at me steadily, but I built a defense system that never let them go too deep. I started at home with my mother, three older brothers, and a younger sister. My mother favored each child differently and for different reasons. I felt abused the most by my mother, and I have valid reasons for feeling this way. Preferring to preserve my mental health rather than to take advantage of the amount of money I was still entitled to forced me to build my own life outside the home and away from my mother. As a result, I did not enjoy the help my brothers and sister got. Their educational expenses were covered by my parents, and my parents even purchased new houses for them as they prepared for marriage. None of these advantages were in my life. Years later, I heard my brothers and sister complaining about my mother, but none of the abuse they received from my mother came close to the abuse she showered on me. And after I grew up, my mother was older, less patient, and unwilling to accept me as an adult.

My mother is nothing but a self-centered person, an overbearing and manipulative person with no emotional feelings of love toward me but plenty toward herself. I cannot remember ever waking up to find peace and happiness. My mother wouldn't let me be. It was as if she found glee in trying to tear me apart. I concluded that her happiness derived only from hurting me and watching me die with the pain. At that time, I would not say she failed to break me. She almost broke me. I hardly saw any good in myself, and I felt like a sack of shit; I wish now that I had known earlier how to practice self-affirmation so I could have bulletproofed my mind against her cruel treatment.

I went through endless trouble with my mother as a child; our relationship never worked out no matter what I did or tried to do. There was distress at home all the time for me. I never heard the words "I love you" from my mother's mouth. There was never a happy nickname for me, but she used word to describe me in bad terms. She would say things like, "The day I knew I had another boy was the darkest day of my life." "I wish you on my enemies." "I did not give you up for adaption only because I did not know what people would say and think about me." She never used sweet words when speaking to me, only plenty of abusive words, belittling me and comparing me negatively to others. This followed me through my life, and even still negatively affects me today.

Despite being discouraged by my mother cursing me day in and day out and wishing all the worst things anyone could wish on a person, I managed to make it through grammar school and boarding school and then go on to college and graduate as an engineer. My life journey was nothing but a series of challenges. Every day brought a new challenge. Getting through it was one of the hardest things I accomplished. It was a long, hard struggle for a small child and later as a teenager.

In one way, all my efforts to fight and be accepted never successfully came through; in another way, however, acceptance was handed to me on a silver platter. A whirlwind of thoughts have run through my head. There is still a long way to go before I get there, and I will tell you all about it if only you can wait to read the following chapters.

My Mother:
Savage and Egocentric

I would like to describe the kind of mother I was taught a mother should be before I describe my mother.

The love of a mother is often described as unconditional and selfless. A mother's love for her children is strong and enduring, and it can be one of the most powerful and influential forces in a person's life. This love is often characterized by a deep sense of protection and care for her children. A mother may go to great lengths to ensure that her children are safe, healthy, and happy, and she may make sacrifices in her own life to provide for her children's needs. The sense of nurturing and support can also characterize a mother's love. A mother may offer guidance and encouragement to her children as they navigate through life's challenges, and she may provide comfort and support during difficult times.

In many cases, a mother's love is a constant presence in her children's lives and can help shape their values, beliefs, and behavior. A mother's love can be a powerful force that helps shape the people that her children become.

But I never felt any of this; I felt only despair, hate, comparison, and absence of acknowledgment. It was as if I was never there.

My mother was the firstborn child in her family. She subsequently had two sisters and two brothers. According to her stories, her mother's method of upbringing spoiled her. She wasn't allowed by her mother to have responsibilities or help around the house. She was raised like a princess and acted that way as well. Her parents backed her up whenever she disagreed with her siblings; in other words, they had to respect whatever she said.

As a child, I watched my mother settle arguments among her sisters and brothers. None of them dared say a word after my mother gave the final instruction or contribution. I guess she had it in her personality to dominate people and be emotionless about the feelings of others. She never had to go through the experience of not having something go her way. That probably explains why she never had any feelings toward anyone.

My mother would push my father to do things he had no intention of doing. She would decide what was suitable for him to do. My father's personality was way different from my mother's. He had a warm personality and expressed lots of emotions toward others. He was a very modest person. All he wanted was to go to work, come home, relax, and read the paper. That did not match my mother's intentions for him. My mother pushed him to go places and meet people, to become a member of various organizations in which he had no interest.

In a way, she made him move forward in his life and become something. She needed us—her children—for her focus. We, as children, did not have our father to spend time with us because he was not home with us, especially with me. When I was born, my father worked at a high level in the municipality where we lived. He had to spend hours outside the home.

True, my father was second to the mayor of the third-largest city in Israel. He had a lot of power and gained respect from many people wherever he went. It was suitable for my mother to be the wife of such a figure. Unfortunately, my father detested that life till he died. While I was growing up, I heard him say he did not want that life, and his actions backed that up. He would say, "Who needs such a life?"

When his wish finally arrived, it was during his last days. He did not want to spend them in banter, and that meant keeping my mom away from him. He did not want my mom by his bedside in the hospital, and he made sure his wishes were honored.

My father died at age seventy-two, much younger than his brothers were when they died. He was the family's pride, and he was well respected, but he did not enjoy his life despite all the accolades he received. I remember my father as a figure of no authority in the house. Most of his arguments with my mother ended when he gave in to keep the altercation from going further; he wanted his quiet.

I have never been able to think back to my experiences with my mom in my childhood days and come up with anything good related to her. Many nights I have asked myself what I did to deserve to be born to such a lousy mother. I never could figure it out.

It can be challenging to cope with a mother who is cruel or abusive, but it is important to remember that it's not your fault if your mother is cruel, and you deserve to be treated with respect and kindness.

The relationship I had with my mom was very difficult, and I wanted to get out of it. Getting out of an abusive relationship with your mom may be difficult, but it is not impossible. I took steps to shield myself as I sought mental health and stability. I set the appropriate boundaries, practiced self-care, and found healthy ways to manage my emotions. I didn't have many friends, but the ones I had were helpful and provided support. They were my friends when I was in distress. You, too, can seek support from trusted friends and family members. Or you can join a support group and meet with others who have had similar experiences. Remember that you are not alone.

My Childhood

I understand that we cannot control other people's feelings about us. I have come to understand that some parents treat some of their kids differently from the way they treat others because they need someone to blame for their problems. Or maybe one of their kids reminds them of something they hate about themselves, or they feel competitive with that child for some reason.

I wish I had known this as a child. Maybe I wouldn't have gone through the struggles I went through trying to let other people define my happiness. I am the youngest boy child, and my mom made me feel even younger and of little value. She never protected me or stood up for me or indicated she was proud of me.

So, it took a while for me to accept that my mother would never stop treating me badly. It did not matter what I did or did not do; the dynamics remained the same. As much as I tried to manage and improve our relationship by trying to go that extra mile, she remained eager and motivated to make my life difficult. As soon as I realized that a mother who cannot be pleased is a mother you should not try to please, I began to save my extra energy for things that would prepare me for the good life I dreamed of having.

Your mother's behavior toward you is motivated by her, not you. Now, if you're making her life more difficult in any way, I would suggest you stop so she doesn't have anything genuine to react badly to. But, if you're acting appropriately and doing your job, stop comparing the way she treats you to the way she treats others. Her treatment may not seem fair, but it will not last forever. You'll eventually be an adult, and you will decide where to live and what to do with your life.

If I were you, I'd make sure I was doing what I was supposed to do. I would envision a wonderful life for myself and start working super hard at building a wonderful life in which I would be loved and cared for without trying too hard. If you're used to being treated poorly, being around someone who treats you well can be great. Your parents are not going to change, and if they do, live to forgive them, but still live your life. I should have just lived without thinking about impressing my mom while I was growing up. But I didn't, and the outcome was disastrous.

Boarding School: Love Is Where You Least Expect It

My first day at grammar school opened a new era for me. My mother was happy to see me go every morning. She did not hide that she was glad to be rid of me for the hours I spent in school. I had difficulties during my early years in school. My mother never showed any favorable emotion; instead she showed only discouragement and uttered only bad words when my grades were down. It made me unhappy and wished I could do more. My mother described me as a lazy student even though she provided me with no support to do better academically. My brothers had no patience with me. They were busy with their own interests. My mother never became involved in helping me, so there was no one to help me through school.

I knew I had to help myself. I stayed back after school hours and read with the students I had identified as brilliant. They were brighter than I was, and there was no point denying that. I tried to be better for my mom and with no success or hope at succeeding with her, it was time to be better for myself.

Today I realize how much my struggles paved a way for me, but that is beside the point. My brothers had no patience for me, and there was no way they would help me through school. It must have been the genes that govern self-centeredness that they inherited from my mother that influenced them.

When I finally finished grammar school, it was time to decide where I would continue my schooling. With only low grades to show, the choices were minimal. Thanks to my dad's connections, I was lucky to be accepted to a boarding school. When I started at my new school, the best thing was being away from my mother. Imagine that! How many people do you know who say such a thing? I felt like a boy among other boys, equal to everyone in every way. That was a brand-new feeling. It took some time for me to adjust. It was difficult, a task by itself.

All my life, I had fought to be recognized and valued in my home, but in the dormitory, I found that there were many people who had more esteem for me than I had for myself. I was noticed, seen, and appreciated. The love I had been seeking was given on a platter of silver. I still had lots of struggles in school, but somehow I managed to get through them easily without having to think of a mother who belittled me. Boarding school gave me a new look at my life. I believe that much of my achievement later on was the result of my experiences at this school.

I was fourteen years old when I moved to boarding school. I must say that the idea came from one of my older brothers, and I thank him for that even today. The idea was to keep me away from my mother. This was a big turning point in my life. Things turned out positively, and it was as if life took a new turn I didn't even know existed. I was among other kids, and I was treated as their equal. My mom had often made me know that I was never going to be equal to other children. She had said it so many times that it seemed like an anthem, but soon, boarding school began to teach me that I was just as good as the other kids. My mother had lied to me to get at me for something that wasn't even my fault!

Life at school was a challenge for me to face. My past made me feel far from being like all the other kids. My background from home with my mother taught me that I was nothing but trouble, nothing in me was positive, but the other way round. I was nothing but distress, and my place was not in this world.

It was a big challenge to be among other kids my age. At first, it felt like a life sentence. I didn't feel I belonged. I felt as if everyone was fooling me, which was not true.

Going away to school felt like another of the manipulative tactics my mother used on me. The challenge was more than just being moved to a new school. It took me a long time to adjust and become like the other kids in the school. I gave up many things I wanted as if I did not deserve them because that was how my mother raised me. Kids took advantage of me along the way. For many years, I thought no one should listen to what came from my mouth. My mother ignored me in every possible way during this phase of my life too. Well, I wasn't expecting so much from her. As a student, it was hard for me to learn. My mind was not engaged, and this made things even harder. Somehow, I managed to get through three years. The good thing that came out of boarding school was that I started to feel better about myself and life in general. I spent these years learning about agriculture, and at the completion of my studies, I started preparing to write my exams for college.

My time at boarding school proved that we can find love in unexpected or unusual places. People may meet and fall in love while traveling or through mutual friends or people at work. Or they might fall in love with people they meet on online dating platforms. Love can happen when and where you least expect it, and it can often be a surprise when it does. When it happens, embrace it.

Many factors can influence whether or not a person finds love in a particular place or situation. Some people may be more open to new experiences and meeting new people, while others may be more reserved and less likely to meet someone in an unexpected place.

Ultimately, the idea that love can be found in strange places is a reminder that love can happen in many different ways and circumstances. It is important to be open to new experiences and not to rule out the possibility of falling in love in unexpected places.

I found love, but it was not the kind of love I was expecting. Nothing would ever have prepared me for its arrival.

My College Years

My years at college were the most essential and most complex challenges. I never faced as many challenges in my life as I did in my first year at college. I started college in a foreign country, learning a foreign language. I had little knowledge.

I come from Israel, which is not nearly as rich as New York. There were plenty of things in New York that I had never seen or even heard of—huge buildings and crowds of people on the streets. Everything looked big, like nothing I had seen in Israel. All the richness and glamour, name brands, stores, fancy cars, and limousines overwhelmed me. I did not know how to express myself, and I could not put words down expertly at the time.

The branch of the college I attended was close to Columbus Circle in Manhattan. I walked from work, which was on 3rd Avenue, to the college. For the first few months, I took the same route to college, and each time, I kept seeing different views that hadn't caught my attention the last time. Each trip was a new experience. I started taking different routes daily so I could discover more unique places. It was amazing to see so many new places I never thought existed. I was impressed.

Unfortunately, I had no one to share my experiences. I was able to share them only with family members in Israel during infrequent phone calls. Arriving at the college was another task to face. The college was in one of those gigantic buildings, and the classes were located throughout the building. The first challenge was to find the numbers of the floors and the classrooms as I walked through the school.

As I walked into a classroom—one that I was not even sure was the correct room—I staggered. I saw many students, and I heard them speaking unfamiliar languages. There were people from different parts of the world speaking all kinds of languages. I had no clue what they were saying. I tried to find someone who spoke English to ensure I was in the right classroom. I don't think he understood me, but I was certain I did not understand him. I took a seat far in the back of the class where I thought I belonged. While I was waiting, a tall skinny person with long hair walked in and started talking as he erased what was on the blackboard from the previous class. It took me some time to realize that he was the instructor. He then proceeded to teach mathematics, and I supposed the students laughed at his jokes once in a while.

I did not understand what he was saying or teaching, but I watched the expressions on the faces of the other students and laughed when everyone giggled. In my mind, I thought that I had made an enormous mistake taking this challenge. Besides, mathematics was not my strength, and trying to understand what the teacher was saying made it even more difficult. I restricted myself from walking out of the classroom and going home, never to come back. Instead, I reminded myself that this was just a challenge, and like the others before it, I was going to ace it.

This was just the beginning of my challenges. If I failed, I would go home after college to face trouble. Getting through my studies was a task by itself. It was not a simple process. I had to first consult the dictionary for the meaning of the words—not every word, but most words, especially the big ones. It got to the point where I knew approximately where to put my fingers on the dictionary page to find the information I needed.

I could spend an entire weekend studying only a paragraph or half to three-quarters of a page until I got an idea of the text. It felt as if the effort was not worth it, and that became my agony of going through college. At times I was not able to understand the subjects, especially computer science. One day I turned to a friend I knew from Israel and asked him to wait for me outside the class. I handed him my test, and he walked me through it. I thought I was brilliant when the instructor returned the test and mentioned that only three students had passed—I was among the three!

But just as he was going to hand me my paper, he said, "You were cheating!" And he ripped it up. I looked at him with a half-smile because I did not understand the word *cheating*.

College was no fun. I had mixed thoughts about my experiences there. My determination to prove to the world that I could make it kept me going to graduation.

I have noticed that it is difficult for people to believe in you and actually accept that you are better at something than they are. People enjoy watching their mates struggle. I knew I would not have it easy, but I put in the work because I understood where I was coming from and where I was going. The margin in the life I had at the time and the life I wanted was so wide, just too wide.

It is not uncommon for people to feel jealous or envious when they see others succeed, especially if they have not achieved the same success. However, it is important to remember that everyone's path in life is different, and it is not productive or healthy to hate others for their accomplishments. It is more productive to focus on your own goals and work toward achieving them rather than dwelling on the successes of others. Additionally, it is important to remember that we all have different strengths and abilities; what comes easily to one person may be more challenging for another. Success is subjective, and it is important to celebrate the successes of others and be supportive of their endeavors. From my experience, I will share with you how you can overcome your childhood trauma.

When I understood how difficult my childhood had been, I realized success was the only remedy for all the hate I had received. I decided to find a way to overcome the pain I had gone through while growing up. It was not an easy task, as overcoming childhood trauma can be challenging, but it is possible with the right support and resources. Here are some steps that helped me in overcoming childhood trauma:

- **Seek therapy:** Even though I could not afford a therapist (or even knew what a therapist was), I was consciously invested in helping myself get better by learning to forgive my mom and let go of the hurt I felt and all the pain she caused me. I had to heal from the effects of trauma. I sought to understand my experiences, identify coping mechanisms, and develop healthy ways of dealing with difficult emotions. I did this on my own, but a professional therapist would have been helpful.

- **Practice self-care:** Taking care of your physical and emotional well-being is an important part of the healing process. This may include activities such as exercising, getting enough sleep, eating well, and engaging in activities that bring you joy.
- **Connect with supportive people:** People who are supportive and understanding can be a valuable source of strength and comfort as you work through your trauma. Surround yourself with these people.
- **Engage in activities that promote healing:** Many activities can help you heal from trauma such as writing, creating art, making music, meditating, and practicing yoga. Find activities that resonate with you and help you feel more connected to yourself and the world around you.
- **Seek support from a trauma-specific support group:** Joining a support group with others who have experienced similar traumas can be a powerful way to feel understood and supported.

It's important to remember that healing from trauma is a process, and it may take time. Be patient with yourself and seek the support you need to move forward.

Marriage and Divorce: My New Life

D ivorce is often a painful and difficult experience that can significantly impact an individual's emotional and physical well-being. It can be a time of intense stress, sadness, and grief as people come to terms with the end of their marriage and the changes it brings to their lives.

One of the most common emotions experienced during a divorce is grief. This can be grief over the loss of the relationship, the loss of shared dreams and goals, and the loss of a familiar way of life. It is common for people to feel a sense of sadness and disappointment as they come to terms with the end of their marriage, and a sense of loss and loneliness may accompany these feelings. I was very familiar with these feelings.

Anger is another common emotion experienced during a divorce. People feel angry with their ex-spouses, themselves, or the circumstances leading to the end of the marriage. This anger can be directed inward, leading to feelings of self-blame and guilt, or it can be directed outward, leading to conflict and bitterness.

In addition to these emotional effects, divorce can have significant financial implications. Depending on the specifics of the divorce, individuals may be required to pay alimony or child support, or they may have to share assets with their ex-spouse. This can lead to financial strain and uncertainty, particularly if the divorce significantly changes financial circumstances.

The social and personal implications of divorce can also be significant. People may feel a sense of shame or stigma associated with the end of their marriage and struggle with feelings of isolation and loneliness. Divorce can also affect people's relationships with their friends and family members, and it may be difficult to maintain or rebuild these relationships after the divorce.

Overall, the pain of divorce can be intense and long lasting, and individuals may need to seek support and help. This may include therapy or counseling, a support group, or friends and family members who can provide emotional support. Taking care of one's physical and emotional well-being during this difficult time can be crucial for finding peace and healing after the divorce.

Divorce has significant emotional and financial effects on both parties involved, including men, but I felt the heat the most during my divorce. The end of my first marriage was difficult and stressful for me, and I experienced different emotions, such as sadness, anger, and grief. I felt a sense of loss and worry about the future, especially for my children and my relationship with them.

In terms of financial conditions, it was expensive and resulted in a significant change in my circumstances.

The divorce affected me psychologically as it affected my physical and mental health. Studies have shown that men may be more likely to experience negative physical health outcomes after a divorce and may also be more prone to mental health issues such as depression and anxiety. I am glad I met the right woman after my divorce. She helped me get better, and she became my peace.

I now face a fresh start. My ex-wife ensures that my children do not want anything to do with me. When it comes to evil work, no one could do a better job than my ex-wife. She tried to paint an awful picture of me, and unfortunately, she succeeded. I believe my kids thought of me as a loser who ran away from responsibilities. In reality, I did all I could to be in contact with them, but I was always turned away by my ex. No, I did not run away. I had no other option. I had planned to come back.

I decided not to go back after learning more about my ex-wife's barbaric behavior when I hired a private investigator to go to the places where she worked. It has become apparent that I will have nothing to do with her again. No, I would not return to my miserable life with her now that she had found a man.

When I got to understand her twisted mind and her outrageous, vicious way of thinking, I would have been better off burying myself in other things that required my time rather than come back. My assessment then to stay in Israel fight for my rights was to avoid to good chance of living a tragedy. I put my concerns for my kids before my concerns for myself. I worried about them being all alone with their mother. Now the kids are grown up, but they are not able to think independently. In agony, I watched from afar my kids' lives play out like my own childhood.

My ex-wife's characteristics and talent for manipulating and fabricating stories without a basis in truth caused the kids to depend on her. She distanced me from the kids so she wouldn't have to confront the truth. My ex-wife has been feeding whoever listens to her with all sorts of colorfully fabricated stories about me. All the while, I am some six thousand miles away with no way to confront her or express my side. My daughter Pauline cooperated all along together with my ex-wife against me because she was manipulated to believe the stories her mother cooked up.

My ex-wife never stops fabricating immoral stories about me. These stories ruined my kids' perception of my love and care for them. She created great distance between me and my kids. I tried to connect positively with my kids, but nothing worked to my benefit. I never missed any birthdays, and I always sent presents. I asked people I knew who were traveling to the United States to hand the gifts to my children. I even went as far as publishing a book so they could know my part of the story and how I was thrown out of their lives as if I didn't matter. I made sure they got to read the book.

The endless efforts to come to some regular communication with my ex-wife led to nothing. My ex-wife lies as a way of talking. She continued to lie, and people sadly believed her lies. I faced an unsupportive marriage both from her and her parents. They were hiding information from me and continuously manipulating me. Luckily, I can now share my story with my readers. I am in a position to be able to let my emotions out and continue with my current life in pursuit of happiness.

Tales of My Wife's Twaddle: My Nonbiological Second Daughter

I love my children so dearly, and even when my wife took them away from me, I fought for years to gain custody of them. I couldn't get custody, and even when I tried to get shared custody with my ex-wife, that proved too difficult.

When my wife had my second daughter, I noticed something odd about the baby. She wasn't like the rest of us. Her skin color was different, and so was the color of her hair. In my excitement, I didn't think too much of it and just fell in love with the newest addition to the family. As years rolled by and dirty secrets began to surface, I can say I was a victim of paternity fraud—a painful and difficult experience for me. A child who wasn't mine was forced on me, and I couldn't face the emotions I felt when I found out. It led me to a lot of emotional difficulties, and I struggled to find myself. I felt a sense of betrayal and was hurt by the fact that I had been misled about the child's paternity. I felt a sense of responsibility to provide for the child financially, even if she was not biologically related, but despite my kindness, she and her mother made life difficult for me.

It was a source of pain and confusion. I felt a sense of betrayal, and I struggled with identity issues as I learned that the girl I believed to be my daughter was not biologically related to me.

My wife had a child outside the vows of our marriage despite the fact that we were still legally together. Being as alert and emotional as I am, my ex-wife's lies and manipulation did not work well for her. During her pregnancy with our second daughter, she had complications that she wouldn't let me know about or discuss with me. She tried to keep me away from what was happening and hid her medical difficulties.

I cared for her and wanted to share her pain and ease her from every difficulty that her condition must have exerted on her. My intention was only reasonable as I did not know what she was hiding from me. During her first pregnancy, her doctor became very friendly with me. The first pregnancy had been all natural without even a single complication.

You may ask how I figured my ex-wife became pregnant outside of the marriage. It was more than evident. She was going through different troubles during this pregnancy, which was unlike her first all-natural pregnancy. She had many more follow-up doctor visits with her second pregnancy than she had during her first pregnancy. We used to drive to the doctor together, but I was allowed into the room with her to hear what the doctor had to say only on the first visit. For other visits, she refused to let me in the doctor's clinic while they talked. I waited outside in the lobby, kept in the dark, unaware of what was happening or what the doctor was telling my ex-wife. I knew the doctor from the time of my sister's pregnancy. He was very friendly, yet he kept me from the complications my ex-wife was going through.

I remember going to the hospital unexpectedly at the doctor's order. I prepared to be with my wife while she gave birth naturally, as she had done with the first. At the hospital, the situation became very urgent. My wife was rushed to the surgery room for a C-section. I waited outside until the surgery was over. When the baby girl was born, she looked quite different from my first daughter. Her skin color was different. She didn't look like mine because she was white. My first daughter and my son had darker skin tones. She also had other variations that made me confused. Her hair color was not like any in the family. I tried to think of family members I thought she looked like, but I found none.

As she grew up, this girl acted weirdly in many ways. None of her behavioral patterns were like mine, but she distinctively had a personality in sharp similarity to my wife's. As time passed, it became evident that my wife had this girl outside the marriage. I brought up the question in a way that allowed her to admit it. I was willing to accept it and continue.

However, the fact that she lied troubled me. The more I asked, the more she got panicky. I felt that was my natural right to take a DNA test. That was the straw that broke the camel's back. Needless to say, throughout the years, the subject kept coming up. Quite honestly, at that point, I didn't care anymore.

I felt bad that my ex-wife never admitted to the girl that she was not my biological daughter. That girl experienced mental challenges throughout her life as a result.

Over the years, I made endless efforts to get to my children. However, whenever I got started to get close to them, my ex would distance them from me. For twenty-five years I did not know anything about my children. I have spent more years away from them than with them. And it hurt not to be allowed to play my role as a father in their lives. I didn't get to know much about each one's individual personality than what I already knew when my marriage broke up. They don't care to know about me. Later in my life, I felt angry with them. I live well, thank goodness. I managed to have a beautiful second wife and children. The loss of my love and care for my kids resulted from the distance my ex-wife created. I made endless efforts to connect positively with my kids, but nothing worked to benefit the children or myself.

The endless efforts to establish some everyday communication with my ex-wife led to nothing. Pauline was fourteen years old when the divorce took place. Pauline and I had boundless love and an excellent father-daughter relationship, but after the divorce, my ex-wife poisoned her feelings toward me. I used to speak with my daughter on the phone, and she told me countless stories about how I had been terrible to her and harmed her. She repeated all kinds of made-up stories that she hadn't even been aware of as a child, obviously the repeated malicious tales told to her by my ex.

The Mind of Evil and Chaos: How My Ex-Wife Thinks

I spent sixteen years with my ex-wife, enough to learn about her personality. My years with her made me an analytical clock that was always carefully calculating her moves and actions. I can describe her feelings, knowing they were only a part of her personality. This chapter will describe how my wife thinks and her perspective on things. The next paragraphs are words my wife said outright. She owned up to her feelings and wasted no time in actualizing every bit of them.

> I would dump my husband and marry another person. Then I could do whatever I want. That is what I want, and that is what I have achieved. My personality is that way. I know what others don't know, and I do whatever pleases me. I betrayed my husband, cheated whenever it paid me, ignored my kids, and left it to my husband to take care of them.

> Yes, I had him change their diapers, get up at night to care for them, and help them with homework. He bathed them, cooked, and took care of the cleaning of the house. Above all, I insisted he take on three jobs aside from the flea markets on weekends and delivering newspapers weekly on Friday night. This man did not know how I packed away hundreds of thousands of dollars all from his labor. Whenever he asked where

all the money was, I would throw a tantrum until he gave up.

As time passed, he stopped asking me. Yes, I was a bitch to him because I could sense his resentment of my behavior. He comes from a well-known family with lots of morality, whereas I come from a family with nothing to show as an accomplishment.

My father works in the produce department as a clerk at the supermarket. He kept moving from one position to another. He was caught stealing money from the register and putting it into his pocket. My mom worked at the bank doing all kinds of tasks to keep the job going since she had no education in any field.

On the other hand, my uncle and my aunt were much better off. My uncle was an educated man who worked as a bookkeeper, and my aunt was a schoolteacher. My family did not believe in school or education. My brother and I did not go through grammar school or the ten years of schooling mandatory by law. We dropped out with a big thank you from the principal. Of course, to get a job as a bookkeeper, I managed to lie and say I had a degree. Better yet, I did not have anything to show other than my word.

I love taking advantage of others' trust in me while I target them for my plan, not for their benefit but for mine. The way I see it, it is easy to get people to believe my fabricated stories. I quickly get people to trust me and go with it. If I get caught, I keep people satisfied and move on to the next task.

When my employee saw me taking money from the cash register, I paid the money back to keep my husband from finding out. My actions caused me to hold nearly a dozen jobs on Long Island. I embezzled money wherever I could. I managed to pay our bills at home from the money I got at the places I worked.

Boy, did I screw businesses, but I couldn't care less. My husband and kids were my most effective tool to use for all my tasks. My ex-husband stayed with me to be with the kids. He loves them and was willing to overlook my immorality to remain with the kids. Knowing that gave me the leeway to do whatever I wanted.

I took out of this marriage enough to move on to another man of my liking. I must have raised between $3.5 to $4 million. Please don't ask me to tell you where all the money is. I don't even remember. My ex-husband insisted on being a member of the Jewish community center. It is so ridiculous that he went there while I was hiding tons of money. But anyway, my husband helps generate money for the temple to pay for our membership by volunteering several times a month at bingo.

I had him work extremely hard and never showed him any appreciation. Instead, I made him think he was not a good provider. Should he complain, I would turn the story around, make him believe he is paranoid, or shut his mouth using my talents. I have now been away from him for twenty years. I made sure the kids hated him and didn't want anything to do with him.

I dumped my ex-husband and married a person I could do whatever I wanted with. That is what I wanted, and that is what I have achieved.

My ex-wife wanted things to go her way, and she didn't mind who she pushed or who she used to get what she wanted. She didn't care who got hurt in the process, and most disheartening, she didn't care who she ripped apart because, if you were in the way, you were going to suffer dearly for it. Her motto is: My family at my command.

I wasn't sure my mom had a motto, but my ex-wife was just like her. I eventually moved from having peace to living in a fury hotter than I had read of in books. It was now my experience, and for once, I wished I had taken more time to pause, think, and get wisdom from those bumper stickers I had seen in New York.

Finding the Angel

In most fairy tales, the fairy godmother of the enslaved princess appears waving her wand, and eventually, the evil stepmother pays for all of the mistreatment and takes back the evil words she has ever said to the princess. I quickly discovered that my life was not heading in the same direction. I had waited my entire life for something good to happen, and as a child, I wished over and over that my own fairy godmother would simply appear. Yet, as I grew older, I came to terms with the notion that there was no godmother. Oh! The entire fairy tale series was nothing more than fiction written by exceptionally gifted writers. She is not real.

I was well past the age of believing in fairy tales when I realized that something beyond my comprehension was about to fall into my lap. When my life began to mirror the picture portrayed in the book that all youngsters cling to as they grew older, I realized that mine didn't have anything to do with a fairy godmother. It wasn't some story an exceptionally talented writer could have put together either. I can't help but draw attention to several significant exceptions to my story because I am still having trouble trying to wrap my head around them.

For me, I sensed God beaming down from the heavens, succinctly rewriting the story of the shattered boychild who grew into an even more broken man. My sole mistake was being born a boy, but I don't think the mind of the one rewriting my story regards that as a mistake when he looks at me. I had been trapped in a deception for most of my childhood, but I felt a grip stronger than that lie dragging me out layer by layer. I desired freedom my entire life and was unable to resist it when I felt a tingle of it in these firm hands. I realized quickly that I had to come to terms with the truth in this new story he was writing. It wasn't a mistake at all! God had intended for me to be here, and the timing of my arrival couldn't have been more perfect.

This arrangement was beyond anything I could comprehend. As an engineer, I had learned to be quite analytical, yet what happened on the train to the Rockefeller Center eluded my analytical prowess. Tossing aside everything I had ever known and following the power at work felt like a struggle for me, but that is exactly what I did. It was the beginning of a transformation, the change I frantically searched for but couldn't achieve on my own.

My first contact with the angel was on the train we shared to Rockefeller Center, yet something about him pulled me in, and our relationship grew beyond just being fellow commuters. I was planning to go back to Israel that day, and I needed a miracle to make it possible. I have shared the story in the previous chapter that convinced me that it was necessary for me to go back to where I was raised—not back home with my mom, but to familiar surroundings where I might find the kind of future I wanted. For some reason, I had the impression that my good life was in Israel.

He had a level of patience that I had yet to witness in anyone else, and he exuded a calmness that made me feel both vulnerable and unafraid. I won't go into all the intricacies of what happened between this man and me. I initially thought he was an angel, but our first meeting was so carefully orchestrated that I think it is unreasonable to leave those intriguing details out.

I had bought a ticket at the airport, but I didn't have a passport. I was on my way to the passport office via subway. My journey from the airport to the subway station provided me with ample opportunity to reflect on earlier occurrences in my life. The trip to the subway station was the longest I had ever taken, and every curve and bend in the road made my insides turn with uncertainty. Turmoil roiled inside me, and I felt as if I was plunging into a familiar darkness. My stomach ached just thinking about it.

I got on a crowded train that I wasn't even sure was the right one, but for some reason, I didn't bother to ask anyone. Regardless of the number of eyes that watched my every movement as I entered the train, I managed to find a comfy seat. Once seated, I let myself unwind in the one source of comfort I had at the time. It was going to be brief, but I was going to relish it and just blank out to escape reality. I knew I would eventually have to face this darkness, but I wished I knew exactly how to beat it and make it go away.

The train stopped at a station, and some commuters got off while new ones swirled onto the train. The man sitting beside me got up and made his way out of the train. I was indifferent and watched the new commuters scurry around for comfortable seats. I waited to see who was going to sit in the now vacant space as we all took the thirty-minute trip together; for some, the trip would be shorter. Then I saw a man walking directly toward the seat beside me. It struck me as odd because, unlike other commuters who had done a quick search with their eyes for a seat, this man simply walked in with his head to the floor and came toward me as if the seat had been reserved for him. Even more strange, I am not sure anyone thought to take the seat beside me before the man came directly to take his spot. Perhaps they hadn't seen a vacant seat there.

He appeared to be a simple, uncharismatic man, and he had his head covered to show his allegiance to a religious tradition. It stirred some curiosity in me, and I leaned over to check out the leather bag he was carrying. Of all the things neatly tucked inside the bag, my eyes settled on a big Bible resting as if it was at home. My eyes lingered longer than I intended, and for reasons I still don't understand, my first communication with him was to ask him if he would lend me his personal Bible so I could read some of it. He graciously complied by removing the book from his black briefcase and giving it to me. Those moments were not the way I had envisioned my trip to Rockefeller Center, but as I learned after I got to Israel, they would define the next fulfilling years of my life. The gear was changed, and that was where my life took an interesting turn.

I decided to ask this man who had been kind enough to share his Bible with me if I was on the right train. I told him where I was going, and he confirmed that I was on the right train. I asked where the best place to get off the train was, and he said Rockefeller Center. I didn't know where I was going, and I wanted to keep quiet as I had been when I got on the train, but something about him kept me talking. At that moment, he seemed to me to be someone knowledgeable about the area, so I wouldn't get lost following his lead.

I asked him if he knew where the passport office was, and he said he was on his way there. Imagine my luck! If I had made up my mind not to ask him any questions or speak to him, I could easily have gotten lost. As it was, we would be getting off at the same location and proceeding together on foot. I told him I was trying to get an emergency passport to fly to Israel. He looked at me and said he was one of the people in charge of issuing passports. He didn't specify which part he took, and I didn't ask further. I saw that as a reason to focus on the journey ahead.

My heart had begun to beat quickly, so I put my hands over it as though to stabilize it. Since our chat began, I had been looking into his eyes. They appeared very calm. Something in them gave me the impression that I could trust him. My feelings had better be right!

I can't exactly remember the part of the Bible I read that day, but this angel took charge of things from that point. I had boarded that train with no expectations, but because of his involvement in handling things, I was able to obtain a passport that would be my way home to Israel. For most of the time, this angel called the shots, and I stood in one position, transfixed and, at times, trying to figure out what was going on. The more I tried to find a logical explanation, the more I kept making a fool of myself. My bid to find an explanation had taken me out of real time, and the questions this man asked forced me back to reality.

At the exact time I needed my passport to be issued, a passport officer sat next to me on the train. This was a miracle that God put in my lap, and at that point, my current darkness just didn't look so dark anymore even though it still felt heavy and difficult to comprehend. The tension in my chest began to loosen, and then it suddenly dropped when he told me I had a meeting scheduled for 2:30 that same afternoon. Everyone had said I would ever get my passport before my flight at 6:30 p.m. Yet there I was with a mystery man who only had to place a single call to a number I didn't even know!

There was a kind of peace that radiated from this man, and in a split second, I found myself recounting again the past occurrences of my life to him. Right there in the waiting room, with my face buried in my palms, I cried like a baby. I don't know if I was relieved that someone was finally listening to me or that I was finally able to get the big lump off my chest without being interrupted.

Not once did this man cut me off, and everything about his body language made me know that he was following. He constantly held my eyes, and each time I looked into his, I saw compassion, support, and peace, just peace. I had never felt this kind of closure, and after my father died, I longed for a man I could share my burdens with or have a good rapport with. I wasn't just looking for a random man; I was looking for a man I felt could fully hold the position of a confidant. I had just met this man, so I couldn't make any hasty decisions yet, but this man stood taller than the bridge I had built to prevent anyone from coming too close—the bridge I knew how to construct so well.

I was a bit sorry that the first thing I shared with this man was my burdens, but he didn't seem to be bothered. He gave me the time I needed to tell my story, cry, and gain back my composure.

That one experience convinced me that I couldn't lose contact with this man. I have a difficult time welcoming new people into my life, and even now that I am a much older man, that hasn't changed much. This man caused the defenses I had built around myself to fall like a pack of cards, and I was soon exchanging numbers with him. I had to keep in touch.

We had only one conversation after my experience with him that day. He called to learn how my flight went and how things were picking up for me. I wasted no time in letting him know that I was making a fresh start, so things were a bit rough but not beyond what I could handle. And as he had come into my life, he disappeared again. This made me really wonder if he was even human. I didn't even know his office location! Whatever help he rendered that day in New York all happened on the spot. I didn't have to go to his office as I thought I should so that things could be more official.

At his disappearance, I tried to find closure for my children, but each step I took brought me to a dead end. It hurt so much that I wouldn't be able to be a part of the biggest and littlest achievements in their lives. Every means to get through to them was blocked, leaving me with hope.

Numerous disappointments came after that, but the contact I had with this man was too solid, and I couldn't shake off the feeling that God had his eyes on me, and he was going to show up. I lived each day with high expectations even though life seemed to have other plans. I was stubborn too, fighting back and protecting my body from the physical defects life came to deliver. This was the only thing I knew, and I wasn't going to give it up so easily. It was going to be a fight to the finish.

I was desperate to fill the void that had been forcefully created. I wanted to give my children the experience of a father figure, so I was on the lookout for anyone who could relieve me of the emotional trauma my experiences had caused. My father had been an ideal provider in every way, but I didn't connect with him much because of the demands he needed to attend to with regard to his several businesses.

As a child, I felt that void mostly when my mother started with her constant complaints and insults, and this happened more often than not. My father's constant absences almost made me feel as if I grew up with only one parent. Each time he came home, though, there was always a positive aura he brought with him. His manliness made things quite different. I know the void Papa's absence caused, and I didn't want my kids to feel that way—not with a mother who was a replica of my mother. I would often think of my life as a child and be full of dread for my children. My face was often creased with worry.

Thoughts of my wife having sole custody of my children sent dark shivers down my spine. I remembered the times I had curled up in blankets because I thought my mother was an evil empress waiting to rip me apart. I remembered the days when I stayed in the closet and hid because I was too scared to face her. I remembered how, as I grew older, I stayed in school for long, unnecessary hours after class because I didn't want to go home. Away from home, I was safe. Most parents protected their children from the world outside the home, but outside was my safest zone. What an irony of life!

I had made sure that my kids were never afraid of anyone before my marriage crashed and the court gave full custody of the kids to my wife, but that was when they were pretty young. Would they still know that years later? How much damage would Charlotte do?

I would sit in my armchair and ask questions about my kids: What are they doing now? How is school going? Are they as bright as I remember them being? What is their mother telling them about themselves? Are they getting the same encouragement I would give them when they failed at something growing up?

My list of questions was endless, and soon I would drift to sleep slouched in the chair until the morning sun and the chirping birds came to wake me. There was a bright-yellow bird that always stood by my window and sang. It never left until I opened the windows again. His song was a call from creation to come back to reality and live my dream, to fight to get my kids back.

My second wife, Priscilla, was supportive throughout the entire process, and I am grateful to have her. We were married by then, and though she had every right to be furious at me, she never did. She didn't even feel a hint of jealously or bitterness. She knew how important connecting with my children was to me, and she never once stopped fighting beside me. She never knew them beyond the pictures I shared with her and the stories I told her, yet her eyes were full of admiration and love. She always said that the way I fought gave her more assurance that she could trust her kids with me. She saw more of a husband, father, and friend with each passing day, and that boosted my esteem. It gave my ego a bit of a boost—not ego to flex my masculine muscles, but the knowledge that a woman needed me and felt safe beside me.

It was as if her hands wrapped around mine giving me more self-awareness and making me want to do more. I couldn't give up, and she made sure that I didn't even though the children in question weren't hers! She didn't feel threatened, and neither did her own three kids. They always longed for the time when I could bring my kids to Israel so they could become friends and make closer bonds than the pictures could ever offer. Disappointment laced their faces each time bad news came, the same news they had been hearing for the past few months.

I had written dozens of letters to organizations. I sought justice organizations, organizations for fathers' and children's rights, as well as social workers dealing with abused children. During some weeks, I sent out between ten and forty registered letters around the country in my desperation requesting assistance. I didn't know how far my letters were going, but I was willing to stretch beyond the places I knew. I would remember how cruelly Charlotte had pulled me away from our children's lives. I resolved that every effort was worth my sweat and time. At least one of my letters would get to the right desk, and the right processes would begin.

I was desperate to connect with someone who could help me ease the emotional pain I was experiencing from being estranged from my children—someone who could help me secure custody of my children or at least some visitation rights. But no help was forthcoming. I didn't get full custody, and it proved more difficult than I could have imagined getting shared custody. Moreover, the systems were being upgraded with each year that passed, and each year my efforts proved more abortive.

My discovery of new system updates and processes made me feel cold down to my feet. Sadly, I found that a father's devotion, love, and grief weren't enough to reconnect him to his children. Even worse, his sweat and time meant nothing when the system weighed money as a more valuable transaction consideration.

In the midst of these circumstances, I knew I had to find the angel again. I hadn't done enough when I had tried to search for him the last time. He had told me his name and given me his cell number, but everything had changed in so short a time. I searched every possible place for him and called every number I thought could have a connection to him. What was supposed to be an easy task proved rather difficult. Then it hit me!

He had mentioned the city where he resided, so I did a thorough search based on that location. I soon realized that this frantic search was leading me nowhere. I think I turned over planet Earth in search of this man who had become my friend in the shortest time interval, but there were no traces of him. Days ran into weeks and weeks into months, yet there nothing worthwhile came up about him.

I turned my attention to the media, but even that proved a weak means for finding this man. My enthusiasm began to dwindle, and when Priscilla, my wife, noticed, she decided to step in. Heaven blesses the day I met this woman because she knows exactly how I feel every time. She can smell my mood from meters away, and I couldn't be more grateful that she came into my life.

Priscilla soon began to dig deep, but the dead ends were more pronounced. She found the same name and background information, but they didn't give further information about the man I had met. She would sit all day looking through information about people who shared a similar name with this man. Perhaps there was a link or something in their profile that could help us find this man. She even went as far as contacting organizations that had the responsibility of searching for lost people. She stressed herself around the clock, and I began to talk to her about dropping the search. When she wouldn't budge, I encouraged her in the best way I knew how. Months slowly tickled into years. Then the long-awaited information sprang up.

Priscilla came to me with a picture she hadn't yet seen in all her searches. She was certain this had to be the man, and it took only one look for me to confirm that he was the one. The swell of excitement that came through from her was my satisfaction. The search hadn't been futile at last.

I immediately reached for my phone and dialed his number. My heart jumped when I heard his voice. I recounted my story to him to help him remember who was on the line. My excitement almost overtook me, but my task was to ensure that he remembered, and he did. He asked me to keep our conversation anonymous so I wouldn't be sharing the details.

At the end of the call, I checked through the information we had gotten about him through Internet searches, and a lot of other things popped up. I found that he was part of a significant world organization and functioned as chairman of the board of several prominent organizations.

We had scheduled a meeting, and I couldn't wait to see him. A feeling of comfort enveloped me as I ventured on the journey that would reunite me with this man. The meeting was scheduled in his office, which was located in the most-guarded facility in Tel Aviv. It was in one of the major companies where he served as chairman. I passed through numerous security checkpoints with strict security protocols that, in my opinion, were impenetrable. My identification card was among the things I had to put in a box. I expected to arrive to find a man sitting in a spacious office, gazing out at Tel Aviv through his large windows.

He had given me the proper direction to the floor where his office was. I took the elevator and made my way there. The elevator opened into a reception room. The table was made with fine marble and glittered beneath the crystal chandelier. Different lights in the room gave it a cool ambiance. I was warmly received by a lady who was dressed in tailored pants and a sleek jacket to go with it. Her smile was broad, and I almost assumed she had a description of me to confirm my arrival to the angel, but I guess a policy must be in place to treat everyone who stepped into the office with the respect she displayed. I took my seat in the air-conditioned room and waited in anticipation for the slightest glimpse of this man. Different emotions took hold of me, one of which was excitement at seeing him again. I began to rehearse the lines that I had articulately put together so I could show gratitude for the last time he had rendered his assistance.

My thoughts were that any man in such a position should have had a contingent of personnel to wait on him, but to my surprise, the angel appeared alone from his office and came directly toward me. I don't think I was expecting that he would show up himself to escort me to his office. There are no words to describe the modesty of this man. I expected to see a man dressed in a nice, fancy, tailored suit, polished shoes, and a matching tie. He instead was dressed in a nice, clean shirt and denim trousers.

At the sight of him, I began to rub my hands together. The words I had rehearsed quickly started to evade me. I had already stood, but now I was disappointed as I fought to remember my lines. He gave me a huge hug, making the few words of appreciation I could recollect hang in my throat. That hug was sincere and held every indication of support and love. I still feel that hug today. He walked me to his office, which was not as large as I had pictured. It was just enough to accommodate a desk, a phone, and a room for two or three additional people. He was modest in every way. He said not a word about his achievements in life, and he had lots to share if he had wanted to.

First, we discussed the day we met on the subway in New York and how he had helped me obtain my passport against all possibilities. Without him, the process may have been incredibly long or even impossible. I believe he had contacts. At this realization, I cannot but wonder what made a man of his social status board a public train. I didn't understand his simplicity either. I believe he felt more comfortable being behind the scenes than in the limelight. He enjoyed his peace just being treated like every other average person in society. Although I doubt he would be treated as such by those who reported directly to him. Only a person of his significance can pass through all the bureaucracy. He must have had connections at the highest places.

Don't get me wrong. I have known people who have supported me along my journey of regaining my self-worth, which had been stripped from me before I even knew what it meant. I had little or nothing left to turn to by the time my mother was done with me. I have experienced positive relationships that have helped rebuild the walls that were fractured—walls left vulnerable for anything and anyone to sneak in and do more damage.

A friend in college was the first person who ever showed me true friendship. Regardless of the walls I had tried to build, Gabriel kept reaching out, and I began to unconsciously let down the walls I had built. It wasn't unthinkable to let down my rigid boundaries just so I could let him in a little bit. Though I was still a little guarded, I gradually popped my head out from my hideout, my comfort zone. I came out only when I was sure that it was safe enough.

Gabriel made life less difficult for me, and soon I noticed that I felt comfortable sharing my laughter with him. Maybe I could not share my tears and deepest emotional scars, but I was able to freely laugh around him. I have mentioned in previous chapters how associating with people was tough for me, but Gabriel taught me that not everyone was out to hurt me. No one could blame me much. I had established strict restrictions for allowing people into my space because of the treatment I had been given at home. I just felt that, if my mother could be that bitter toward me, maybe I was just really bad. I didn't think it was possible to get the love I desired outside the walls of my family. The moment you are out of the security edge around you, you are exposed to danger. In my case, my home wasn't a security zone, and everything in my gut doubted that that security could be found elsewhere.

His laughter was so carefree, and he had a friendly nature. He could get me rolling in laughter in almost a split second. I wondered if he ever had any worries, but if he did, he never showed them. Maybe because of my proximity with him, I could detect those moods, but they disappeared from his face as soon as they showed up. I wanted to be like him, but I knew I would have to make a conscious effort. I wasn't sure I was going to make it because I still had to go back home and listen to my mother's complains and rants.

Gabriel cleared my fears and made me discard my negativity in the trash. I owe my ability to open up to the angel to him. I found something in this man that was more than what I saw and felt in Gabriel, but Gabriel had been the link that made me receptive to this man who defined my life in our brief contact.

I am grateful for many people like Gabriel, but I only wish now that I had been more open. Perhaps, then, I would have had more friends I could run to for assistance. I knew a few of my course mates who have now climbed to the top of the societal ladders, but there was no basis for a connection that would warrant my ability to reach out to them for help. I know better now because, even though the angel just a man, he walked into my life carrying a bag of possibilities.

Gabriel was kind, but far kinder was this man, this angel.

Gabriel was really humble. He was the best student in the class and usually had no fierce competition. He bagged A+ grades in his classes, yet he walked with little indication of his academic achievements. Perhaps it was because I was struggling with most of my courses and couldn't easily figure out how to get it right. He never shoved it in my face that he was the brightest in class and I was way below his level. Rather, this brightest of students held hold my hands and taught me to write, read, and solve arithmetical problems. He told me to get rid of my mentality that convinced me I was too dull to understand. I wasn't as dull as I had allowed myself to believe. The moment I began to strip off that mentality layer by layer, my grades began to rise.

Never have I seen a friend so happy at my achievements as Gabriel was, and he even set up a full reading plan for me. His aim was for me to pass him in most subjects. I didn't think I could do it, but Gabriel thought I could do it. He also had listed a thousand and one things he knew I could do; there are not enough the pages in this book to list them. He had a mantra he said out loud each morning with a smile on his face before we stepped out for classes. He didn't force me to say it, but he didn't chide me for not believing too. He said I would come around, and I did.

I had been saying it a lot, but on one particular morning, I stood with him in his favorite spot in front of the window. He gave me a bemused look, slapped me a high five, and rumpled my hair in a friendly way. He did that often, laughing as I fought to protect my well-combed hair. He asked me how I felt saying his mantra, and I responded that it was okay. My outward response was a bit shallow, but deep down, I knew that saying this mantra was the start of something new, a shift.

I soon started standing by the window every day to say it with him. As I later grew into adulthood, I lost those positive feelings, and I forgot the mantra. But the presence of the angel brought back a lot of positive emotions and revived my memory.

Oh! The mantra?

The world is yours to take.

That was Gabriel's mantra, and it is my mantra.

The angel wore his humility like a cloak wrapped around him, from the way he walked to the way he dressed and his conversations. A man like that must have made a number of top achievements, but he didn't think once to mention them. The conversation never at any point spiraled to him. I have met people who would talk briefly about themselves and others who would completely forget the topic of conversation we were sharing. Whatever time I had left with them after a brief explanation of my situation would be spent talking about who they were, the ladders they had climbed, and the people they knew. I would leave their offices feeling more dejected than I had when I arrived.

I had made no spectacular achievements, and I knew nobody. I was still struggling to get my children back from my manipulative wife. I had a broken marriage. It wasn't difficult to see that these people had sweet marriages. They didn't miss mentioning that in their conversation. I would listen and then walk out the door with my head down.

This was one of the things that made me open to the angel. He never talked about who he was or what he had achieved. I don't know the reason behind that, but I am grateful for it. If he had been different, our relationship would have been short lived. He gave me every reason to want to find out more about him, and the moment I did, I was awed to be in association with such a man. He didn't seem like a stranger anymore; rather he felt like a father (even though he was not many years older than I), a brother, and a friend. With the space my father left, it was good to let someone I admired fill the void; I found him the most appropriate person.

Reconnecting with him would be one of the best decisions I had ever made. Now I had that association to always run to. Ah! The wisdom this man possessed. I have yet to meet anybody who was as wise. The angel had a solution for every situation I took to him. His body language was responsive, which made me feel as if he was wrapping me in a hug when he hadn't even moved. His eyes held understanding and compassion.

I was conscious of the fact that the angel was not just any man. He was an important dignitary, and I had to be mindful when speaking to him. When he noticed me stiffening my conversation with him, he told me to loosen up because he was just like everyone else. I didn't think he was! I don't think even now that he is! He will raise objections to this, but I just can't see him in any lesser category.

I made several life-changing decisions after my meeting with the angel. There were fascinating things about him that I just wanted to replicate in my own life. His manner of approaching people who were of a lower social class was full of humility. I am not trying to sideline people and remind them of where they belong within society. I am just trying to explain that this rich, classy man cared little about status. It wouldn't be out of character to find him talking to a beggar or assisting an elderly woman cross the road safely. Such was this man's life, and I wanted such simplicity in mine as well.

Years spent with him made me realize that I was not nice enough or kind enough. I started working on these areas where I knew I desired a change that people would benefit from. I took a stance to be nicer, kinder, and more lovable to everyone. I wanted to be a shoulder to many who didn't know me, just as the angel had been for me. I felt I could lean on him even when I had barely met him. Just one contact should be enough, and I was going to learn enough to see that happen.

There are things I know now that I wish I had known then. My life would have taken a different turn. But having gone through experiences and picked up a series of lessons from them, I can share with young, middle-aged, and even older people how to live a more rewarding life. My marriage took out chunks of me during the first few years, and even at that, I felt that I could cope with the barriers it brought. I remained and gave up my happiness for the benefit of others. My dream to let my children live with the presence of a father became shattered before it even started. I became like a grieving woman who had been separated from her child even when the pain from childbirth could still be felt.

I am a man and can never know the degree of that pain, but without my children, I felt naked for many years. I didn't think Charlotte deserved anything good from me again, but with my new resolution to be better, having learned from the angel, I often included a gift parcel for her when I sent gifts to my kids. I don't know what she did with them, or if my kids even ever got their gifts. I determined to live right, practice peace with all people, including my ex-wife, who continued to make life a living hell for me.

I had a lot of questions. I played out scenarios from the past and realized I could have handled things better. Maybe I should have done things better, but in a real sense, did I not do enough? Did I do too little to satisfy Charlotte?

My healing came with a lot of exposition, but rather than take on self-forgiveness, I blamed myself a lot. I felt I should have handled things better, but Priscilla kept ensuring me that I had done my best. That position, though, was a place I needed to get to myself, and the journey was stressful. Realization hit me that we are all responsible for our actions, and so was Charlotte. She lived off making a mess of peoples' lives, and I was no exception. She wanted to treat me poorly despite how well I treated her. She was like that, and there was nothing I could have done in a thousand years to change her. There were areas I saw in myself that I needed to improve, but I shouldn't take the blame for a ruined walk I tried so hard to save. Charlotte just didn't want it saved. She wanted out, and she was going to have it her way.

The angel acknowledged that my hurt and pain were valid, but he explained that I am responsible for my happiness. The angel became a kind of therapist even though I didn't pay for that kind of service with him. I never paid for the second visit to him or even several others, but each time I walked out of his office, I dropped layers of anger, anguish, and pain. I don't understand the effect this man had on me, but he wielded his knowledge well.

I needed to heal, but it came at a cost. I had to be intentional and seek peace and happiness. It didn't happen in a year, and I admit that the same hateful feeling came even after progressive journeys down this path, but I had to intentionally let go. I began to loosen the rigid boundaries I had set that prevented people from coming too close, though I didn't live without them. I just had to ensure they were healthy boundaries not built out of shame or even prejudice for female folks.

After the abuse from my ex-wife and even after I married Priscilla, I didn't associate with females. But by letting go, I started opening the door to building genuine friendships with them. I have two sincere friends who are like mothers to me. They share bits of advice that their years of experience have given them. Many tips have helped strengthen the bond I have with Priscilla.

I had to learn trust again, and Priscilla made the entire process easy for me. She was very understanding and took things a step at a time. When I felt disappointed at the feelings that overwhelmed me when I thought I should have let them go, she constantly reminded me that it was a process and I had been doing so well recently. This woman coming into my life is the best thing that has happened to me, and I cherish every moment I spend with her. She showed patience and love at extreme levels, and at times when she needed to tell me things sincerely, she never lost the respect she has for me.

My first marriage may have been bumpy, but I understand that this woman deserves the best of me, and walking through healthy mental processes is a step toward her getting all of me. Yes, I was battered and injured, but the journey to find freedom was mine to take. Going back and recollecting and then intentionally shutting the door on every pain inflicted may not have been the most pleasant experience, but I have built a family with a different mindset and theology. I have learned to be more positive and step out each day with a positive expectations. There are many more stories about my life, but let's leave them and focus on you.

You need to go back and address certain issues before you can really embrace your happiness. You have to make peace with yourself and the people you have to forgive. Although the path to better mental health may be tough, I can guarantee you that it will be worthwhile.

I have learned to walk each day with grace. With an adorable family and a blooming business, I have learned that the world is, indeed, mine to take.

I hope you believe that it is yours to take as well.

Israel: Home like No Other

My first family was precious to me. I stayed for a long time in the United States, but finally, I made the decision to return to Israel. Although during marriage, life was brutal and unkind, I never took the initiative to go back to Israel. Going back to Israel meant breaking up the family, which was not my intention. I felt very much responsible for my children. In reality, I stayed in my awful sixteen years of marriage only for my children. I lost any feelings toward my ex-wife thanks to the way she treated me, her general behavior, and her endless lies and manipulations. Besides, she had been hiding my money and other valuable things for years, such as the gifts my parents had brought for my children.

She hid essential information that came through the mail. She was a monster throughout our marriage. It got to the point that there was no use in asking her anything. I knew the answer would be another fabrication. During my twenty-one years in the United States, it came to my mind too many times to return to Israel. I discussed starting a new life in Israel with my family members at times; however, they advised me against the move whenever I mentioned the possibility. Usually, I was told that it was not the right time to start a new life in Israel. The economy was terrible, and there were no jobs available. I received even more discouragements.

I consider myself a survivor. As a survivor, I chose to make the best of the marriage situation, hoping and praying it would change. We had three children, and they were my good reason to try even harder. Besides, we had a three-story house on an acre of land, two late-model cars, and a boat. As far as comfort goes, I had no reason to complain.

But that didn't make my general feelings and soul happy. One thing led to another, and sixteen years went by.

I hardly remember one day when I felt happy. Luckily for me, my ex-wife started a secret relationship with a man behind my back. My ex would have gotten much more from me if she had acted like an average human. No wonder there is a saying, "you get more with honey." I guess that applies to our everyday lives and people who want to work out their differences with their partners and children.

Despite her inhuman acts, I was willing to discuss with her the best communication strategy between me and my children; after all, I had stuck to the marriage for the children. I must admit that she thwarted my efforts to contact my children. The amount of alienation and bad-mouthing me in front of the children was unbearable. I realized that my ex-wife did not intend to reach a middle ground.

Furthermore, she wanted to destroy me even more, as if the separation from my children was not enough. I then decided that my life had to continue. At one point, I felt that there was nothing more to do, and that was when I published the first book, in which I shared my story and my message to my kids.

After so many years abroad—twenty-one years to be exact—returning to Israel was not easy. After all, I had lived my maturing life in New York. Because I was alone during that time, I had to be tirelessly focused to survive. Eventually, I learned to think and do things like any ordinary American if I wanted to survive and make my future there.

My understanding of life in America is way different than life in Israel. The language, style of dialogue between people, care for others, the taste of food, the type of culture, and even the way of kidding around with others are different, and values for both material and spiritual aspects of life have different meanings. Adjusting again to life in Israel after years of being away was no easy task. That is because I was traumatized at the time. I had to deal with my children being away from me. That was very hard. I could not go back to live in the States after my ex-wife stole all my assets including the money we had accumulated over the years.

My ex was on the move to destroy me even more. She hoped to put me in an institution, making it look as if I was the crazy one. I understand that her motive was to cover up all the negative fabricated stories she had built about me to the kids.

Today, being away from her, I can see how well things turned to my advantage. The experience of my first marriage and my divorce was awful, but I was able to do a lot of things with my time alone—things I didn't think I would have been able to do if I was still in that marriage.

Being away allowed me to think and realize what kind of a woman she was. I realized that my wife didn't mind having a life in which I was not present. As a matter of fact, I think she had removed me from the picture a long time before I realized; I was too blind to see it. And when I saw it, I stayed because of my children. It was meaningless trying to make my marriage work while my ex-wife had another life of her own. My ex-wife acted behind me to secure a life with everything I had built, but in doing this, she gave me the chance for a new life.

So, coming back to Israel had its advantages after all. The first year was somewhat traumatic for me. By the second year, I started to get back on my feet. I found a girlfriend to share my life with. I purchased the essential items to get into the job market doing gardening work. The marketing and sales job was easy since my sales background came from New York.

Life after the divorce started to pay in a big way. I never forgot my children and tried on occasion to make contact. As the years went by, my efforts intensified until I realized that my determination was one sided only.

Life after Divorce

Let me share with you my ex-wife's point of view on the divorce. This chapter describes how my ex-wife is "proud" of her lifetime achievement. It is unfortunate that she sees her behavior as an achievement, but no one else sees it that way. She is a self-centered person. Does she realize the damage she caused herself and our kids, let alone me? After my divorce from her, I learned that life is more than taking my ex-wife's muck every day, and there was no shortage of slime coming from her.

I recognized that life could be a pleasure and fun. I made new friends and shared my happy time with them. I am creating a new and better life. It would have been an utterly fantastic life if my kids could have been around to share those positive moments. My kids will never learn about my love and care for them, and that remains a scar I can't brush off. It will remain with me for years and maybe even forever.

I had my ups and downs during the years after the divorce until I settled and managed to continue with my life. As I mentioned, my life turned out much better than it would have if I had continued with the marriage. My kids suffered from many negative consequences because of my absence because, when I was with them, I would have never let their mother control them and turn them into puppets the way my mother did to me.

My second daughter, Michelle, and my son, Paul, are under psychiatric care. My kids are unstable, and that has greatly affected their behavior. My son has become overweight. To my knowledge, he has gone through several gastric shortening surgeries. My second daughter doesn't know who her biological father is, and living that way is destroying her mental state. My older daughter, Pauline, never found the "right man for her." She grew up with a mother who complained about every man she bought home. I grew up the same way with my mother complaining about the women I dated. Now that I think of it, I think Pauline being born a girl might have been disheartening for her mother too. My mother would have sorted and planned out my life if I had let her. My ex may have wanted to plan and arrange a marriage and maybe rigid family planning schemes that she thought befitting of her daughter.

Pauline is about forty years old and divorced from a marriage of only seven months. She had several relationships with other men, but they never materialized into marriage. She always discovered terrible things about all the men she met.

Luckily, my divorce from Charlotte did not affect my life with the exception of my inability to see the kids. I must say that the divorce from Charlotte is the best thing that has happened in my life.

I was able to get back to living a normal life like the one my father dreamed of while he was on his deathbed. I became healthy and financially secure. I have lived a good life in every aspect. The years after the divorce taught me what I don't think I would have been able to learn without going through that experience. Those years after that marriage gave me a huge opportunity to carefully choose everything that I would not have been able to see or learn had I stayed married.

I feel like a happy camper. I am now at that stage where everything seems to be excellent. I have a wife to back me up and children who respect me. I finally feel like a head of a family again. I am a man whose presence means protection, love, care, and providence to a beautiful wife and three lovely children. I take care of my obligations and have fun watching them sacrifice a lot just so they can give back to me as well. The kids love and care for me. I lost contact with children I loved dearly and fought to keep by my side. I fought for their attention and fought for their love, but with my new family, these things came effortlessly. This was the kind of love I learned from my aunt and wrote of in detail in my journal.

The pages of the journal are so worn out now, but I don't need to go through them again to know what was in them. I learned to love myself. All the members of my family show in actions and in words what love means to us. It wouldn't be surprising for a stranger to spot the nest we have built over time. We are a tight knit family, and everything I know to give now started when my aunt decided to show me what I had never experienced—love.

I am talking about myself and how I have become such a solid person after surviving a difficult childhood and a bad marriage. Despite that, I have ended up a happy camper, and I am grateful day in and day out.

This book will teach you how anyone can make it through life. It is so easy to give up, yet life is more important. I lost twenty-one years of making millions of dollars in one single day. Despite it all, I now feel like the happiest person on this planet.

The Investigation

For the sake of my future as well as my children's, I wanted to correct the injustice that I had been dealt at the hands of my ex-wife. Although it was financially taxing for me, I hired a private investigator to run a check of all the places Charlotte had worked as a bookkeeper on Long Island. The investigator visited two companies listed on Charlotte's resume. The investigative report indicated that Charlotte had been fired from both companies for stealing money.

There must have been a good reason for Charlotte to have changed jobs every few weeks when we were together. I strongly suspected she had been stealing money from virtually all her employers. I knew she had stolen money from me and some of her former employers, but I would need strong evidence to sue her and recover the money.

It would be a long, expensive process, but it would be worth it. I wanted to obtain access to the vault shared by Charlotte and her mother where I believed they had hidden money, valuable jewelry, important documents concerning my privacy, and other items of importance. I also wanted to know what had been reported to the IRS as my income during the past years and why my residence was on record as being in Pennsylvania, where I had never lived.

With the help of an attorney, I hoped to recover at least some of the money Charlotte stole from me. I wanted to use the money to help my children and fight for my rights as a father. Charlotte had painted a horrible picture of me, and it would take a lot of time and effort to change my children's views of me. Unfortunately, the attorney I hired did not believe my story.

When he contacted Charlotte and listened to her side of things, she convinced him she was telling the truth. He insisted I provide more concrete evidence to the contrary. Of course, it would be impossible to recall every event over a sixteen-year period or analyze her behavior while we were together. To understand her motivation, I would have to think the way she did, but that was something I was never able to do as I do not understand her logic.

But one thing was certain. Charlotte had an agenda right from the get-go. She knew exactly what she was doing over the years. She had a game plan that was preplanned and well executed. She was ruthless and manipulative. I knew this would make my fight for justice difficult, but I would never give up.

Charlotte was enjoying her life with my hard-earned money, and I was determined to do whatever I could to regain what had been lost.

A few years ago, I attempted to find my daughter, Pauline. I contacted schools and colleges. I also searched the Internet for the email addresses of my children. After I received an email from Pauline, we started to communicate. I sensed the emails were not from Pauline, and soon I realized that Charlotte was the one sending them. From then on, I was cautious not to reveal anything about my plans. I couldn't afford to hire a private investigator, but that didn't mean I didn't try to get messages to my children. I wrote letters, but they were destroyed before they reached their hands.

I once asked a woman from the American Coalition for Fathers and Children in New York to forward a letter to my children. I sent the letter to her email address, asking her to please print and hand deliver it to my children at their home. When I didn't hear from her for quite some time, I emailed her to ask if she had delivered the letter.

She replied that I had not told her the whole story, implying that I had lied. My ex-wife had been at the house when she arrived, and she told stories that made me look like the bad guy, and I wasn't around to defend myself.

I had to apologize to the woman, and I never heard from her again until recently. I made the mistake of sending her a mail to enquire about the possibility of her providing an endorsement for this book. She informed me in no uncertain terms that she would have nothing more to do with my plight or me.

I was tired of spinning my wheels and getting nowhere. I desperately wanted to contact my daughter, Pauline. So, despite my lack of funds, I decided to search for a private investigator. Luckily, I found one who turned my life around. He understood my financial situation and was willing to be flexible. He found Pauline and delivered a letter to her from me, telling her how much I love her and how I wished things had worked out better.

Since then, I have been in touch with Pauline at her place of work every week. It has taken a while for Pauline to open up to me because she was hurt. Charlotte had steadily brainwashed her for years. I believe my regular contact with her has brought us closer together. On one occasion, when I called Pauline, the lady who answered the phone recognized my voice and told me my daughters were good kids. Only then did I realize that my other daughter, Michelle, also worked there. I immediately hung up the phone, redialed, and asked for Michelle. It was a thrill to speak to her.

I am looking forward to the day when I can have a face-to-face meeting with my daughters. Of course, I would also love to see my son, but so far, I have been unable to contact him.

My private investigator is also assisting by investigating my ex-wife. At my request, he drove to New York to investigate Charlotte's past while she was a bookkeeper. The surveillance report I received from him was sufficient for me to start a criminal investigation.

My private investigator contacted a criminal attorney and went over the surveillance report with him on my behalf. As it turned out, the attorney was a criminal defense attorney, and he did nothing but sympathize with my ex-wife.

Once again, my ex-wife had thwarted my efforts in fighting for justice. I would not have been able to get this far in my fight to regain control of my life without my private investigator's generous assistance. Words cannot express how much I appreciate what he has done for my children and me. I am grateful to him and his family for their love and support.

Sarah

Sarah is the woman I was introduced to when I ended a relationship with another woman with whom I did not have good chemistry. I liked Sarah's personality and enjoyed life with her as a person. I moved into her house and immediately invested in it so that it increased significantly in worth. I looked for ways to make it comfortable for both of us to live in her house. I did that believing that I would be spending my later years in that house.

It was vital for me to make her home comfortable. However, Sarah's daughter was bitter and saw me as a competition for her mother's attention. Her daughter was very forceful when it came to having her way. I thought that, if I wanted the relationship to work, I must swallow much of her bitterness. That was precisely what she showed me—nothing but bitterness. And I made a mistake thinking that the relationship could work regardless of her dislike of me. Unfortunately, her daughter kept pushing me, and the more I took, the more she was encouraged to make my life with her mother miserable.

She was like some self-centered people I had known when I was growing up with my mother. The only difference was that I could choose to stay or leave. I made the choice to go several times, but the consistent pleas and begging from Sarah always made me return. She made me feel as if she needed me around. I liked feeling needed. In many ways, I did all I could to make her not feel that way, but all my efforts were ineffective.

Life with Sarah and her daughter became unbearable. The events of one fateful day made me rethink what I wanted out of life. I had taken the dog out for a walk, and as we walked along, he was run over by a car. Sarah's daughter blamed me for his death. It became unbearable for me to continue living with both of them. Despite all I had done and all I had invested in remodeling her home—several thousand dollars of my own money—I packed up and left with no intention of returning. I loved Sarah, but life with her and her daughter was not the life I wanted for myself. I wanted peace, and I was going to go out of my way to have it.

I had several short relationships until I met a woman named Priscilla.

Priscilla—A Breath of Fresh Air

My life turned all the way around and became enjoyable. Here is the good part of my life—and the good part of my book. The year was 2007, and it just happened that Priscilla and I met at a forty-plus meeting. Priscilla was a divorced woman with three children, two daughters and a son.

At first, I hesitated to become involved with a woman with three children after being unable to deal with Sarah, who had only one child.

Luckily, Priscilla knew how to work our relationship so that the children did not cause friction. Her wisdom and the tact she used in solving situations made me think she was worth living with. I began to look at her as someone who could build a home. I thought of her as a homemaker. Maybe I hadn't been considering a relationship before, but as I watched the way she pulled the strings, my mind often drifted in that direction. We really respected each other, and life took a turn for the better. My entire life shifted. I was living a new life that I did not want to end quickly. I needed to get used to this life. I must add that a beautiful life is easy to live.

Priscilla is the only child of older parents. She was raised carefully by her parents and received lots of love and attention when she was growing up, yet she does not have the personality of a spoiled girl, which you might expect. We dated for about two years. I went back and forth from my home to her home, but I was eager for communal life in one home since I believe that stability and family-constructed energy are necessary. I used to call her before going to sleep and wish her good night. One night, like every other night, I had called to wish Priscilla good night, but her voice was agitated. Her house was on fire!

She assured me she and the kids were fine and explained that the fire department was working to prevent the fire on the second floor from affecting the first floor. They informed her that an electric shortage must have caused the fire. My instinct jumped in, and in a few minutes, I was in my clothes and driving to her house. I lived in a neighboring town, about a thirty-minute drive away. Priscilla's ex-husband was at the sight when I arrived, and my heart sank when I saw him, but I decided to play cool, act like a man, and help Priscilla in the best way I could. To my surprise, he was mainly concerned about items in the house.

Her ex walked into the house as the fire department worked to put out the fire. He intended to collect whatever he had bought his son.

At the time, I offered Priscilla and her three children accommodation in my tiny apartment. We managed to make do in my small, two-bedroom apartment. I expected her ex-husband to invite the kids to be with him, but that was not the direction of his thoughts.

Priscilla's younger daughter, Beauty, continued at her school traveling by bus from my town to her town every day. Her son was joining the mandatory service in the army. He would visit on weekends and share the living room with his younger sister. I set up one room beside the bedroom for the older daughter, Susan. Having a house full of people was a wonderful feeling, but oftentimes, I worried about what we would eat. Amazingly, we had enough. It was crowded, yet we did our best with what we had. During that time, Priscilla's house was rebuilt.

The contractor estimated ten months to a year to finish and have the house ready to live in. During that time, Priscilla was looking to rent a place. She felt guilty about all four of them moving into my tiny home, but she didn't know how happy I was to have them around. I let her know that she and her kids were more than welcome to stay as long as they wanted. Life continued to be comfortable for all of us.

Priscilla's kids are well behaved. In that little apartment, we learned to live less comfortably but more enjoyably! The kids bonded with each other as well as with Priscilla.

The reconstruction of Priscilla's house took more time than expected. It lasted about two years. During their first year with me,

Beauty finished the remaining school year in the town where had they lived before. Because Priscilla's house was not ready to move back into when the new school year started, Beauty started a new school in the city where I lived. I guess that change made Beauty's life turn for the better. She was amiably accepted among her new classmates. That delighted Priscilla because she was very concerned that Beauty was a timid kid, but Beauty's self-confidence started to increase in the new school.

Priscilla's house was nearly ready to accommodate her and her kids again, but since Beauty was doing so well in her new school, we started to look for a better and bigger place for all of us in the town where I lived. Moreover, Priscilla's parents were getting older, and going to their house was an issue in itself.

Finally, we moved to a new home. It was bigger and more comfortable. When Priscilla's house was ready, we decided to rent it. We all lived together as a family; we had known each other already for seven years.

At that time, Priscilla was diagnosed with leukemia, which caused a significant turn in our lives and relationship. She was hospitalized for over a month in a room by herself in the hematology department. She had to go through a bone marrow transplant. No one was allowed to visit except for her kids and me, and only one person could be with her at a time. Visitors had to wear personal protective equipment. For a month and a half, I moved in with her. I slept, ate, and showered in that room.

Watching her go through treatment was frightening, and I had to be there to watch every process. She was getting medication through her veins that went directly to the central vein in her heart. I would stare at her and wonder what was on her mind. It made me very unhappy to see the woman who had changed my life for the good connected to so many tubes. There must have been at least ten tubes funneling to the main artery in her heart.

During that time, I would get up in the morning, close the folding bed in her room, and sit next to her. Nurses and doctors would come in all day long to check on her and bring medications. It was an overwhelming experience for me. It would be, I believe, for anyone who is not a doctor or a nurse. I spent most of the time in her room. The only time I went outside the room was to go to the kitchen to make coffee.

There I met other people who were accompanying their loved ones. I heard stories that could have only happened within the four walls of a hospital. If people told you those stories outside the hospital, you would not have believed them. People described how symptoms had started and how sicknesses had come unexpectedly. Going to the nurse's station to inquire about a patient was a source of despair for many patients and their loved ones who stayed to care for them in the hospital. While she was in the hospital, Priscilla insisted I go home and prepare meals for holidays. She requested that we gather together; she wanted me to bring her mother to our home.

Priscilla had kept her sickness from her mother, who was an older woman. She hated to have her mother worry about her, so we kept our lips sealed as Priscilla lay in the hospital bed. While in the hospital, we continued having holidays at home and brought her mother as she requested. We still didn't tell her about her daughter's condition in the hospital. Her mother did not even notice her daughter's absence because she had dementia. Priscilla is a noble woman in every sense. She was very attached to her mother. Both women were significant to one another.

Finally, Priscilla finished the treatment in the hospital, and we went home thinking it was all over. During her recovery, she lost her mother. She mourned for her, and I held her during those periods more tightly than ever, and she didn't complain; she said she felt protected.

The journey back to health continued, and she needed to go for regular checkups and take endless bone marrow tests to ensure the bad cells were dead and the new cells from the transplant were taking over. We spent days at the hospital waiting for the results, always hoping for good news.

One day, we waited a long time for an update. When the doctor eventually came out, there was no mistaking that whatever news he had to give us was not good. Priscilla and I knew immediately because his face had already given us most of the information, but we weren't sure we were ready to hear it. We hoped we were wrong. The doctor told Priscilla and me that she had to do the whole treatment again. She would have to be in an isolated hospital room for one month. She pulled me to a hidden vending machine in the corridor after our discussion with the doctor and busted into tears. I didn't know how to help her, so I wrapped my arms around her. Her sobs shook her whole body violently, and I feared that she might become sick. I had seen Priscilla cry only at the news of her mother's passing away. It was a moment of extreme emotions for us, but we would move forward in hand in hand. While she was hospitalized and we faced the unknown, we contacted our family attorney to ask him to rewrite her last testament.

I remember holding her hands to give support. Her hands looked frail in mine, and I tried not to let her see the pain I felt in my eyes. I would often tell her that everything was fine, and we were going to get through the sickness together. I needed to be strong for her—for both of us—even though I felt weak at times. I was always optimistic and kept holding on to her. I assured her I wouldn't let go, and I meant every word of it.

With all arrangements with the attorney in place, we acquired a gravesite close to Priscilla's parents' resting place. There was no way to explain the feelings running through our minds. We were going through this journey together, and sharing her tough days broadened our love and hope for better days.

Fortunately, the good news arrived: the leukemia was gone from her blood cells! However, even now, she has regular checkups in various hospitals around the country, and she sees specialists for the different side effects she has from the transplant. She takes a cocktail of medications daily, which affect her everyday life.

I once had to take Priscilla to the emergency room when she had a fever. She was rushed from the emergency room to the intensive heart-care unit. She spent a week in the facility with proper care and attention, and thankfully, she survived. We had previously booked a trip to Romania for that week, but we had to spend the week in the hospital. I was not allowed to stay in the hospital at night. Every morning I would stop by the nurses' station and see the new list of people who had passed away the previous night. That was such an awful thing to have to do. Well, life has become way different than what I expected. I love her and want to be there for her. I was then, and I still am.

Priscilla's children appreciate my caring for their mother, and that has strengthened my bond with them; they are very attached to me.

Our relationship reminds me what I have missed with my biological children.

A sense of importance comes with being the head of the family. My flesh-and-blood children have no respect or willingness to see and know about me. I truly adore and care for Priscilla's children as if they were my own. I receive plenty of love and care from these children. My life became what I was hoping for: I am part of a loving and caring family. I am the head of that family, and I am treated as such.

We are consistently living alongside the disease and making the best of it. Aside from the disease, we have a wonderful life together. I made a marriage proposal to Priscilla. She accepted. Of course, the kids helped, and we all prepared a modest wedding at home. We all were happy and celebrated the event in a restaurant. It was the beginning of better things to come, and we all showed great commitment to learning more about each other.

I do all I can to help in the house, and in return, I receive care, love, and respect. I have also learned that, once you live an unhappy life, you become someone who just wants to get by each day when you are meant to enjoy every minute and every moment. No one knows what tomorrow will bring. Therefore, we book all kinds of cultural events such as shows and movies. We meet and make new friends and take trips as much as the circumstances allow.

I feel loved and respected. It is common for people in relationships to want respect from their partners. This is especially important for men, as traditional gender roles often place a high value on men being respected as leaders and providers within a relationship. When a man feels respected by his partner, he feels valued and appreciated and can also feel more confident and secure in the relationship.

Respect can be shown in various ways, such as by listening to and considering a partner's thoughts and feelings, supporting his or her decisions and goals, and treating him or her with kindness and consideration. When a man feels that his partner is not respecting him, it can lead to frustration and resentment and may even lead to conflicts or difficulties in the relationship.

It becomes very important for both partners in a relationship to be aware of and considerate of each other's needs and feelings and to make an effort to show respect and appreciation for one another. Doing so makes both partners feel more connected, supported, and satisfied.

This respect is what I get from Priscilla and her kids. Since I met them, my life has been improving. I feel respected and loved by her kids. Priscilla's son and his wife love to visit us on weekends and for Friday dinner. I love to cook and bake because everyone gobbles up whatever I cook, and I love it. I feel happy and lucky after all. I am now at that stage of my life where everything feels and looks fabulous.

My wife and I have mutual feelings toward one another. We feel love, care, and respect, and we are tuned into one another's needs. We are at the age where we are financially secure. We have all we need to live a good and comfortable life; we buy as we need, and we can have anything we want. I am not ashamed to say that nothing comes for nothing. There is a long story behind all that—a lifetime of many new beginnings, including different countries, a disgusting divorce, and an abnormal ex-wife who is competent in destroying her life and taking those close to her down with her.

Our next vacation this year will be to Europe. I had no problem taking off from work to go on vacation. Since I retired, all I do is plan for the next break. I am practically doing what I feel like doing. I could not be in any better situation. So many people I come across complain about all that is going on in their lives. Not me anymore. I endured plenty to get to this stage. I am fortunate to be and feel like "a happy camper" day in and day out.

Although I am not a material person, I must say that we live in a big, nicely furnished house in a highly desired location. We both have new cars. I am not ashamed that nothing comes for me quickly or easily. There is a long story behind my happy life that cost me a lifetime. There have been many new beginnings for me including different countries, cultures, and mentalities of understanding people.

Priscilla's Kids

Things have taken a new turn, and thanks to Priscilla and her children, I now consider myself a family man. As far as I am concerned, the kids are an important part of my life. When I married my first wife, the kids that followed were greatly important to me. I wanted to be around them so much, I was willing to take my ex-wife's lies and manipulations day in and day out. I could not let the family break up and ruin the kids' lives.

The world today is controlled and governed by women. They have more rights and enjoy considerably more favors within the legal systems. I became vulnerable to fighting for my right to be part of my kids' lives and fighting to retrieve half the assets I had built up while I was married. It takes something as simple as a woman making up a story to have tons of attorneys jump on the bandwagon to make money off the backs of poor men. There are many cases like mine worldwide. You may agree or disagree with me. In any case, this is my feeling, my point of view, and it comes from experience.

Priscilla's kids are more than welcome in my life. They are as good as my biological kids, and they relate to me with respect. I don't think my biological children would have been as loyal to me as Priscilla's children have been.

The growth stages of children are crucial, and as they grow, they face many challenges that affect their behavior. I am glad to be a part of the growth of Priscilla's children and to be able to influence them in my way of thinking.

With Priscilla, I now have three beautiful children—two daughters and a son.

Susan, the older girl, has spent most of her time with her biological father. She doesn't feel hatred toward him, but she doesn't speak of him with so much love either. She complained once that her father makes her nervous when he doesn't respect her needs whenever she asks for something. He was a self-centered individual who always thought only about himself. I feel as if that left a big scar on her that she still lives with. Susan is now happily married and lives in Germany with her family.

Priscilla's son, Maxwell is also married and has a child.

Beauty, the youngest girl, is living with Priscilla and me. We have a gathering every two weeks for Friday night dinner. It is a nice, big-table, sit-down meal whenever Susan and her husband visit Israel. We are all cordial with one another.

I feel great to be the head of this amazing family; that is what I wanted and wished for with my ex-wife. That never happened with her, but with a new family and life, I feel blessed.

I am now retired and feel emotionally, physically, and financially secure. I have a comfortable life—the life I did not have before I met Priscilla. I have such peace and quietness and a place to call home.

In the next chapters, you will read about how I have tried and failed. I have run and fallen, and then gotten back up again. I am a resilient go-getter with a never-give-up attitude. I believe there is always an opportunity to start again, to dream again, to love again, and to be happy again. You will read a bit about my experiences and how you can always try again, regardless of your age.

Lessons Learned through Lack of Trust and Blown Fortunes

Trying to remember all the places I have been and the tons of money my ex-wife buried does not make me feel good. I think about how naïve and self-sacrificing I was. I am going to be talking about my businesses, which have grown to be big brands now, and how I started these businesses with almost nothing.

I started with manufacturing jewelry sets, especially for females. My businesses vary. I manufacture custom jewelry, mainly earrings. Contractors handled the manufacturing process. I started by purchasing the raw materials, such as the ornaments, and then sending them to be plated in silver or gold. While this process continued, I moved on to marketing and selling the earrings.

I called on the chain stores all over the country and Canada. I participated in national shows all over the country. Wherever there was one around the country, I built a network through the buyers who visited the booth. I developed a list of buyers from different businesses. For example, a buyer of chain stores with 750 stores would order several dozen of each style for each store, sometimes five different styles per store, at $24 a dozen.

When you multiply the total amount of such an order, it adds up to nearly $90K. Same with wholesalers who would place an order totaling $50K to $150K. At the same time, I shipped orders to vendors in the US, the Virgin Islands, and Canada. Money was pouring in.

On weekends, at times, I peddled at the flea market. Usually, I sold anything that I could get my hands on, like women's shoes, brassieres, handbags, and tablecloths. On an average weekend, I would take $2,500 and more. Money poured like water from the faucet, and even more poured in during the holiday when the take-home was higher. I used to make good money on a good weekend.

The first step toward growing a business begins with what you have. Don't think the money you have is not enough; just start.

Yes, living with a person like my ex-wife was not easy. I felt as if I was living with the enemy. Not only that, there was no support but always discouragement because she complained that I was not a good provider. I did what I had to do under the compulsion generated by my feelings of responsibility toward my children. Breaking up the family would be the worst thing.

My children were the top priority, and that caused me to be the way I was. Unfortunately, my ex-wife realized this and took advantage. I also did not think a person could be as immoral as she was. Growing up, I never thought that people acted in such improper ways, but she taught me a great life lesson.

It can be incredibly difficult and emotionally draining to be in a relationship with someone who is only taking advantage of you. It is important to remember that you deserve to be treated with respect and kindness. Set boundaries and advocate for yourself in these situations. There are a few lessons I learned from my previous relationship even though I learned them the hard way. In a nutshell, you decide what you want out of life. It is then reasonable for you to walk out of a degrading relationship. It can be hard to let go of a relationship, especially if you have shared a significant part of your life with someone. Always remember that you deserve to be treated with respect and kindness, and it's okay to walk away from a toxic or harmful relationship. It may be difficult at first, but it's better to be alone than to be with someone who is only taking advantage of you.

In the next relationships that I experienced, I realized how important it was to set boundaries. It is especially crucial in a new relationship when both parties are getting to know one another. Sometimes, even after familiarity, it is advisable to hold your standards that way. Setting boundaries can help you protect yourself and your well-being, and it can also help you communicate your needs and expectations to your partner. This can include allowing him or her to borrow money or use your resources only with permission or by setting limits on how much time you spend together.

Communication became crucial in all of my relationships. It is important to be honest and open about your feelings and concerns. If you feel that your partner is only taking advantage of you, it's important to express the belief calmly and respectfully. This can help you both better understand each other's perspectives and work toward a resolution. I spoke to close friends and family members about my situation. I got advice and encouragement. They provided the listening ears I needed. In my communication with these people, one thing I did not fail to do was to reflect on what I could have done differently, and I held on to lessons that would help me to build healthy relationships in the future. I wouldn't have been able to build a healthy relationship with Priscilla if I hadn't reflected and picked out important lessons from those earlier relationships.

With Priscilla, it wasn't so difficult to build trust, but I had to learn to let down my guard. I let her know how I felt about things and most especially, my attempt to find my kids, whom I still feel drawn to, and she understood. I never made important decisions without informing her because I didn't want her to feel as if she wasn't being kept in the loop. I became more transparent, open, and easily accessible. Priscilla could almost read me like a book, and this helped build more trust and strengthen our relationship.

You need to understand that trust takes time. Trust is not something that can be built overnight. It takes time and effort to build trust, and it requires consistent action and behavior that demonstrate your commitment to the relationship. If your partner does not trust you, it may be because he or she has been hurt or betrayed in the past. In this case, it is important to be patient and understanding and to work together to rebuild the trust that has been lost.

On the business front, while striving for wealth and success, it is equally important to be mindful of the potential consequences and pitfalls that can arise along the way.

One lesson that can be learned from my story is the importance of planning for the future. No matter how successful we may be in our careers, it is important to have a backup plan to put into place if things do not go as expected. This could include having a solid financial plan and a support network of friends and family members to turn to in times of need.

Another lesson that can be learned is the importance of being mindful of one's relationships. It is important to be aware of the potential for resentment and bitterness in relationships and to work toward resolving conflicts before they escalate to a point where they can have serious consequences. This may include seeking professional help or the advice of trusted friends or family members.

In addition to these lessons, it is important to recognize the value of humility and gratitude. No matter how successful we may be, it is important to remain humble and to remember that success can be fleeting. It is also important to be grateful for what we have and to recognize the role that others may have played in our success.

Finally, it is important to recognize that success is not just about accumulating wealth and material possessions. True success is about finding happiness and fulfillment in all areas of life, including personal relationships, career, and overall well-being. It is important to prioritize these things and to remember that money and possessions do not guarantee happiness.

By learning from my story, you can strive for success and achieve what others think is difficult. These principles are simple, and they are valuable. I know because I have lived through them and experienced them and turned them around. Now, they are working for me.

If there is anyone who understands what it means to start all over again, it is I. I am in a position to describe that feeling. Not once or twice have I had to start all over again, and I can tell you that starting again from a difficult situation or setback can be challenging, but I have always been determined. I took time to process my feelings and allowed myself to rest and recharge. It is important to give yourself time to process your feelings and emotions after a difficult situation or setback. This might mean taking a day or two off work, spending time with loved ones, or engaging in activities that bring you relaxation and enjoyment. Taking a break can help you recharge and gain perspective on the situation.

You can be divorced at forty-four years and still find love; you are not too old. You are only too old to do anything if you believe it.

Your life is only over if you let it be. You can still chase happiness and win at sixty; at fifty, you can still make as much money as you want. In the same way, you are not too old to achieve your dreams; you are not too young either. If you built your business up, and when you are fifty, it comes crashing down, start all over again! I pray it doesn't happen, but it could.

If your relationship crumbles when you are seventy, try again. No rule says it is ever too late for you to start all over again; nothing says you cannot change your life. Only you can say that. You can go back to college at age thirty-five and change your life completely.

Are you currently having difficulties reaching your dreams? You can start now. Do you want to run a life coaching business and be invited to speak at universities? Do it. Chase happiness!

People even change their lives at eighty years of age! So, saying that fifty is too late is like saying that, once you start watching two episodes of a show, it is too late to switch to a different one. Of course, there will be some time you will not get back, but isn't it better to cut your losses at fifty than regret them forever? Even at ninety, you can still change your life. As long as you spend the remainder of your time happy and doing what you love, will the time you wasted matter anymore?

If you think it is too late, I encourage you to look at the opposite instead: Your life can change whenever you want it to, but you must take that first step. Decide you will live an amazing life from this moment onward and take the necessary steps to get it.

The fact is that you are too old to keep waiting for life to change! You must do something now! You are too old not to live the life you want! So, change it.

Epilogue

The beach was pleasant and inviting, but I would have preferred to share the evening with Priscilla. Her room in the hospital had a direct view of the beach, and she had persuaded me to leave the room and enjoy some fresh air outside this evening. She said staying with her all day could make me sick, but I wasn't complaining. Just to see her smile, I grabbed my jacket and went for the door. She is currently going through one of those difficult times, but it will soon be over, and we will be back out enjoying life together. She is learning each day to be a survivor just like me, her husband. I don't know if it is our level of intimacy that has had so much influence on her. She appears more resilient and has thick skin that can tolerate the discomfort that comes with each treatment session. Each time the physicians insert a needle into her, she feels pain, and her face shows strain, but it quickly passes as if it were just my imagination.

The doctors have given us no negative results, and we are optimistic that this phase will pass. She is getting healthier, stronger, and happier.

I looked for many signs of discomfort but found none. I only stepped away from her bedside after I had asked her many questions, observed her facial expressions, and made sure she was comfortable. Every step I took toward the shore made my heart race a little, yet I was also connected to the tranquility that nature possessed, which perfectly described how I was feeling. Priscilla and I have struggled together over the past few years, but our love for one another has never wavered. She doesn't even seem less attractive to me because I still see the same woman I fell in love with every time I look at her.

I sat on the warm sand and allowed the sun to bathe me as I relaxed. I saw a couple of people, most of them young children and teenagers, running along the shore of the beach. A couple stood out amongst the crowd, walking from the other end of the shore. They looked young, perhaps newly married. Some kids seem to be trying to escape the waves by running, but that wasn't working so well. As I observed them, I wished I had grown up in a similar environment given how content they were with their lives. I quickly found myself paused in my thoughts lest I be ungrateful as I recognized that, although I may not have lived that kind of life, I have lived one that has demonstrated the sovereignty of the divine, a touch from a Higher Power, the hands of God, to transform. I sat back, relaxed, at that thought.

Priscilla is a strong woman, and I bless the day I met her. She may not have been my first wife, but I can tell that she loves easily because of the extraordinary sacrifices she makes daily—things that I didn't think women were capable of. I had a negative image of women because the first two I had known had mistreated me. The first was my mother, who gave birth to me and despised me from the moment the lower half of my body came out of her. The second was my wife, who I hoped could relieve me of the suffering I had experienced as a youngster and provide me with a safe haven to come home to every day. She made going home every day a terrible experience for me, and for the first time, I could relate to how my father may have felt about spending extended amounts of time away from home. It wasn't even a place to call home.

When Priscilla came into my life, she was like a teacher trying to erase all those ideologies that brokenness had given rise to. I knew that I had to come out of that phase, and I am glad I did. We have our arguments, but they are healthy conversations that eventually bring us to a conclusive decision. These disagreements don't drive us apart; rather, they bring us closer together and help us understand who we are.

I have the peace and quietness I have been searching for with her, and it has given me assurance that love can be found and experienced. Priscilla is my world, and like the sunshine, she was sent into my life to illuminate every darkness. She came in with strokes of laughter along with three wonderful children who are exact replicas of their mother. They were young when I became close to their mother, but they never disrespected me even when they knew I had eyes on her. When they came to accept me, I found that they had the same personality traits as their mother. She had taught them well and imparted to them the right ideologies.

There is never a day I wake up beside Priscilla that I don't look up to the sky, aware of the benevolence of God when he sent her to me at the right time. Her smile radiates my heart and makes me giggle like a teenage boy. I am getting older, yet it is so easy to feel as if I am back in my youth when I see her, especially when she is seated right beside me. I had a bitter experience that made me forget the jittery sense of love I experienced as a boarding school student, but Priscilla made me feel like a young boy who had heard that love could be found anyplace and now believed it. This love found me in a forty-plus meeting, the place I least expected to find anything good. To remember that I only just dragged myself there makes me shake with laughter. Perhaps it was the higher power that put me in the same place with the angel who dragged me there.

I let the cool breeze hit my face and go through my hair as I took in the smell of the salty seawater. I had a heart free of pain, and with my heart empty and free, I was able to pick out every distinctive sound—the roar of the waves splashing, the songs of the birds chirping above, the breeze blowing through the swaying trees, and the squeals of young children filling their tiny buckets with sand.

As I opened my eyes, I saw the young couple; they were now in front of me looking at the ocean ahead. The lady rested her head on the man's shoulder, and he stood protectively with his broad back straightened, pointing out various things to her while she giggled. Their hands were intertwined, and that spoke of tenderness and commitment, which their wedding bands unashamedly vocalized. My eyes shone, and I looked into the sky, praying for a blissful home for these two.

I had been at the beach for thirty minutes, but I knew I had better get back to my sunshine. I missed her already.

It is going to be a lifetime together, Priscilla. Just you and me and nobody else. Thank God our kids are all grown up now. You have always made me know that I have all your support. I will walk every step of the way you, giving you my shoulders when you need to rest your head. I have committed to you and intend to fulfill that commitment.

Priscilla, with you, I promise to have and to hold you, for better, for worse, for richer, for poorer, in sickness and in health, to love and to cherish, till death do us part, according to God's holy law.

And this is my solemn vow.

Conclusion

In this book, *Misery to Victory*, I wrote about the many challenges and hardships I faced. I wrote about how I ultimately found a path to lasting peace through perseverance and determination. Despite feeling overwhelmed by misery and suffering, I refused to give up and continued to search for ways to improve my life and situation.

I moved from being the most despised child of my mother into an abusive relationship with my ex-wife. I lost all my money, started all over again, and I still found love with a new family in Israel. Through hard work and persistence, I eventually turned misery into victory, finding happiness and contentment in my life.

The journey from misery to victory was not easy, and it required a great deal of effort and resilience. However, staying true to myself and never losing sight of my goals made it possible to overcome even the most difficult of circumstances and find lasting peace.

Whether through personal growth, overcoming adversity, or simply learning to accept and appreciate the present moment, the pathway to finding lasting peace is open to all of us if we are willing to put in the work and determination needed to succeed.

After you read this book, I hope you find the courage to work hard and stay disciplined to start afresh and chase and regain everything you may have lost due to life's circumstances. Believe me, you can start from scratch; it is just another way of starting from experience. Go find friends. I am rooting for you. Find your peace and live it That is the dream.

Printed in the United States
by Baker & Taylor Publisher Services